ACCOUNTING COMPARISONS

UK/USA

Also in this series:

ACCOUNTING COMPARISONS: UK/EUROPE VOL. I
UK, FRANCE, GERMANY AND THE NETHERLANDS

ACCOUNTING COMPARISONS: UK/EUROPE VOL. II
UK, BELGIUM, ITALY AND SPAIN

ACCOUNTING COMPARISONS: UK/EUROPE VOL. III
UK, DENMARK, PORTUGAL AND GREECE

ISBN 0 86349 165 0

© Coopers & Lybrand Deloitte, UK. January 1990.

Reprinted August 1990.

Photoset and printed in England by Flexiprint Ltd., Lancing, West Sussex

INTRODUCTION

Financial accounting practices in the United States and the United Kingdom have often been assumed to be similar. Close inspection of the accounting practices in each country and the underlying accounting pronouncements, however, reveals that significant differences do exist, and many have a material effect on the financial statements of a company faced with reporting to readers in both countries. This book is designed to summarise the major differences, citing the related accounting pronouncements in each country, so that the reader can clearly identify and understand the differences.

The information contained here is not exhaustive, and it is based on conditions existing at September 1989. For example, the book does not deal with the accounting practices adopted by specialist companies, such as insurance companies, banks and other financial institutions. Readers should consult their business advisers for assistance in analysing the impact of the differences in specific situations. Contact addresses can be found at the end of the book.

CONTENTS

CONTENTS

APPENDIX

COMMON ABBREVIATIONS

CHAPTER ONE

DEVELOPMENT OF

ACCOUNTING PRACTICES

UNITED KINGDOM

The presentation and the content of financial statements in the United Kingdom is governed principally by company law and accounting standards (and, for listed companies, the rules of The International Stock Exchange). The Companies Act 1985 contains the overriding requirement that the financial statements of all UK companies must give a 'true and fair view' of the company's state of affairs and of its profit or loss. The Act also requires specific additional disclosures in financial statements relating to the compensation of, and transactions with, the company's directors and management. The Act contains specific requirements as to the format of the financial statements. These requirements incorporate the EC (European Community) Fourth Directive which governs company financial statements. The Companies Act 1989 enacts the EC Seventh and Eighth Company Law Directives, governing consolidated accounts and the regulation of auditors respectively.

Accounting standards have been codified in the United Kingdom only relatively recently. Before 1971, the determination of what was 'true and fair' was generally the result of evaluating individual situations along the broad lines of existing accounting knowledge and existing practice. Custom led to a good deal of consistency in such determinations, but there were significant inconsistencies. The Accounting Standards Committee (ASC) was formed in January 1970, and is controlled by the six accountancy bodies in the United Kingdom and the Republic of Ireland. These bodies are the Institute of Chartered Accountants in England and Wales, the Institute of Chartered Accountants of Scotland, the Institute of Chartered Accountants in Ireland, the Chartered Association of Certified Accountants, the Chartered Institute of Management Accountants, and the Chartered Institute of Public Finance and Accountancy. These bodies act collectively through the Consultative Committee of Accountancy Bodies (CCAB).

The ASC's stated objectives are to develop and propose for the approval of the councils of the governing bodies definitive standards of financial accounting and reporting, which encompass:

- Fundamentals of financial accounting.
- Definition of terms used.
- Application of fundamentals to specific classes of business.
- Form and content of financial statements, including presentation and disclosure.

The ASC consults as appropriate with representatives of commerce, industry and government, as well as with those concerned with financial reporting. Like the FASB in the US, its approach is also structured and deliberate, with emphasis on due process in standard setting.

The ASC issues Statements of Standard Accounting Practice (SSAPs) upon approval by all six CCAB bodies. As at September 1989, the ASC had issued 24 SSAPs, of which three have been withdrawn. Several SSAPs have been, or are in the course of being, revised.

SSAP2 sets out what are considered to be the four fundamental accounting concepts. These are also written into the Companies Act 1985, and comprise:

- The 'going concern' concept.

- The 'accruals' concept (which includes the 'matching' of related costs and revenues).
- The 'consistency' concept.
- The 'prudence' concept (which includes the anticipation of expenses and losses but not of revenues and profits).

The prudence concept in practice tends to be given precedence over the accruals concept.

The ASC has also published guidance notes on the application of certain of the SSAPs to special situations. The SSAPs have been supported by The International Stock Exchange. Exposure Drafts (EDs) of proposed future SSAPs are issued for comment. Unlike the practice in the United States, these EDs are often used as guides to best accounting practice, and they become the basis for some companies to adopt proposed new accounting practices before the particular SSAPs are issued.

Future SSAPs will deal only with matters of major and fundamental importance that affect most UK companies. The ASC may issue a Statement of Recommended Practice (SORP) when there is a need for a pronouncement on a topic that does not meet the criteria for a SSAP. At present two SORPs have been issued, one covering Pension Scheme Accounts and the other Accounting by Charities. A specific type of SORP known as a 'franked SORP' may be developed by outside groups whose work will be reviewed by the ASC. Franked SORPs generally relate to specific industry problems, for example, accounting for oil and gas exploration and production activities.

The ASC may also issue Technical Releases which give guidance on specific accounting issues.

UNITED STATES OF AMERICA

Financial accounting in the United States has developed primarily in the private sector. The volume of US accounting pronouncements is much greater than in the UK, and the provisions in these pronouncements tend to be more restrictive than those in UK pronouncements. The development of accounting standards in the United States, referred to as 'generally accepted accounting principles', or GAAP, is the responsibility of the Financial Accounting Standards Board (FASB).

Before the FASB was created, financial accounting standards were established by the American Institute of Certified Public Accountants (AICPA, or 'Institute'). The earliest US accounting pronouncements were issued by the Institute's Committee on Accounting Procedures. This Committee issued 51 Accounting Research Bulletins (ARBs) during its existence from 1936 to 1959. The Accounting Principles Board (APB) was established in 1959 with an objective of reducing the number of alternative accounting treatments for identical transactions. The Board issued 31 Opinions and many unofficial interpretations during its existence from 1959 to 1973, and these Opinions and interpretations prescribed specific accounting for various types of transactions. Many of these Opinions superseded existing ARBs and changed accounting practices previously accepted.

These changes were not always popular. The APB came under increasing criticism from industry, government and others. It was accused of monopolising the standard-setting process while not representing the majority of the users of financial statements.

In order to avoid the seemingly undue influence of the AICPA on the standard-setting process, the FASB was established in 1973 as a body independent of the AICPA. The FASB is recognised as the designated organisation in the private sector for establishing financial accounting standards.

As at September 1989, the FASB had issued 102 Statements of Financial Accounting Standards (FASs) as well as 38 interpretations and 34 technical bulletins clarifying existing pronouncements.

FASs, like the pronouncements of the predecessor bodies, often represent changes in existing accounting practices. This means that they supersede earlier pronouncements of the AICPA. However, those pronouncements of the AICPA that have not been superseded by FASB action remain in force.

Recently the FASB has established the 'Emerging Issues Task Force' (EITF) which meets monthly to handle current US financial reporting questions on a more timely basis than the FASB deliberations. Although the findings of the EITF are not strictly US GAAP, they represent best practice and are followed by most US public companies.

Although the SEC and the AICPA recognise the FASB as the authoritative standard-setting body, the AICPA's Accounting Standards Executive Committee also separately provides guidance on certain accounting matters that the FASB has not addressed. The AICPA's guidance is generally presented in the form of Statements of Position (SOPs) on particular accounting issues, Accounting and Auditing Guides for specific industries, or Issues Papers. Although the AICPA's views are not enforceable, they are generally followed by the accounting profession. Such SOPs and industry guides have been generally endorsed by the FASB for purposes of justifying an accounting change. The SEC also issues Financial Reporting Releases (formerly Accounting Series Releases).

The four UK fundamental accounting concepts referred to earlier are also embodied in these pronouncements, and, as in the UK, the 'prudence' or 'realisation' concept takes precedence over the 'accruals' or 'matching' concept in any case where there is a conflict.

The primary influence of government on the establishment of US GAAP has been through the Securities and Exchange Commission (SEC or 'Commission'). The SEC is an agency of the US government. It was created by an Act of US Congress in 1934 to perform quasi-judicial, quasi-legislative and administrative functions in regulating the selling and the trading of securities to the public in the US. The general purpose of the SEC is to ensure full and fair disclosure to investors.

Companies wishing to offer their securities for sale to the US public must file a registration statement with the SEC initially, and periodic reports thereafter. Other common events or situations that generally require registration with, or report to, the SEC include:

- Exchanges of securities in a business combination involving a public company.
- Trading of securities on a US exchange or in the US over-the-counter market.
- Tender offers.
- Acquisition of more than a 5% interest in a public company.

These filings generally must include financial statements prepared in conformity with Regulation S-X, which specifies the form and the content of such financial statements. Annual financial statements filed must be audited, and all audits must be conducted in conformity with US generally accepted auditing standards (GAAS).

The Office of the Chief Accountant of the SEC is responsible for the execution and the interpretation of SEC policy with respect to accounting principles, auditing practices, and the form and the content of financial statements filed with the Commission.

The SEC has statutory authority to prescribe accounting standards for its registrants. Historically, however, it has looked to the private sector to provide leadership in establishing and improving accounting standards. It has endorsed the standards established in the private sector by requiring that the statements that US companies file should conform with US GAAP, and also by requiring companies to make those additional disclosures that it believes are important to investors. The SEC's Chief Accountant maintains liaison with representatives of the FASB and AICPA.

Other regulatory agencies also exert governmental influence on US accounting practices. Certain industries in the US (such as utilities and financial institutions) are regulated, and companies in these industries must comply with accounting standards established by the respective regulatory agencies.

ENFORCEMENT ENVIRONMENT IN THE TWO COUNTRIES

The impetus for enforcing accounting standards is generally strong in both countries. As mentioned earlier, the UK Companies Act 1985 specifically requires that the financial statements give a true and fair view. In the United Kingdom, all active companies, including subsidiaries, must by law have an audit by independent auditors. The auditor's opinion must state whether the financial statements give a true and fair view of the state of affairs and of the profit or loss of the company, and also whether those statements have been properly prepared in accordance with the Companies Act 1985. These financial statements must be distributed to the shareholders, and, with certain exceptions, they must also be filed with the Registrar of Companies. Certain concessions are, however, granted to small and medium-sized companies regarding the contents of financial statements filed with the Registrar.

In the United States, the audit requirement is generally contractual, rather than legal. Except for those companies whose securities are registered with the SEC, the only audit requirement is generally the result of either a bank loan or some other financing agreement by which the company agrees to supply audited financial statements. Members of the AICPA and members of the respective UK and Irish accountancy bodies each have similar requirements to adhere to the accounting standards promulgated by their respective bodies.

For companies that report to the SEC, there is a strong enforcement of US GAAP. Auditors must disclose all departures, and the SEC will refuse to file financial statements that do not comply with GAAP.

In the UK the governance of accounting standards by law has been enhanced by the new Companies Act.

CHAPTER TWO

DIFFERENCES IN ACCOUNTING

PRACTICES

INTRODUCTION

The pages commencing with page 16 set out a summary of the major differences between accounting practices in the United States and the United Kingdom. This summary does not provide synopses of the respective accounting pronouncements in the two countries. It covers only the differences between them. Only the *general* rules applicable to each area of difference have been presented. Therefore, this summary should be used only as a *guide* to identify the broad areas of difference. To obtain details of the precise accounting requirement in each country, reference must be made to the text of the relevant US or UK pronouncement. These pronouncements, where applicable, are referred to at the top of each section. Where no pronouncements are listed, the related accounting requirement is not specifically covered by a pronouncement, but rather is the result of accepted practice.

The individual differences on the following pages relate generally to all types of business. There is, however, also a basic difference in the approach to establishing accounting requirements for specialised industries. In the US, the specific accounting requirements for many specialised industries tend to be set out in individual AICPA Industry Accounting Guides and Audit Guides, and in AICPA Statements of Position. The FASB has also issued specific FASs covering financial reporting in certain specialised industries such as the record and music, motion picture, cable and television, insurance, broadcasting, real estate and oil and gas producing industries. In the UK, however, specialised industries are not covered specifically in accounting pronouncements (except occasionally as guidance notes to certain SSAPs). However, specific practices do develop in such industries with, for example, the issue of franked SORPs.

It is difficult for an individual to keep abreast of those provisions in the United States that are currently effective. This is partly because different bodies have promulgated so many different accounting pronouncements, and partly because there is a continuing process of issuing new pronouncements that supersede existing ones. The FASB publishes a 'Current Text' to assist accountants in grouping and understanding the accounting pronouncements that have been issued.

The 'Current Text' integrates financial accounting and reporting standards according to the major subject areas to which they apply. The subjects are arranged alphabetically in sections that are grouped into two volumes. The first volume (General Standards) contains those standards that are generally applicable to all enterprises; the second volume (Industry Standards) contains specialised standards that are applicable to enterprises operating in specific industries. A comprehensive Topical Index appears at the end of each volume. These Current Text volumes are published annually.

The alpha-numeric references in parentheses on the following United States pages are to the General Standards Volume.

DIFFERENCES IN ACCOUNTING TERMINOLOGY

There are many differences in the accounting terminology used in the two countries, and these can be misleading if not recognised. Some of the more common differences are listed below:

UNITED STATES	UNITED KINGDOM
1. Capital stock (or capital shares)	1. Share capital
2. Financial statements	2. Accounts (although the term financial statements is also in widespread use)
3. Inventories	3. Stocks
4. Capital leases	4. Finance leases
5. Net income	5. Profit for the financial year
6. Payables	6. Creditors (may include accruals and deferred income)
7. Property and equipment	7. Tangible fixed assets (the term fixed assets can also include goodwill and other intangible assets and certain investments)
8. Receivables	8. Debtors (may include prepayments)
9. Retained earnings (does not contain any share premium or other capital adjustments)	9. Reserves (includes retained earnings and sometimes share premium, as well as certain other charges and credits)
10. Revenues (or sales)	10. Turnover

UNITED STATES Cont.	UNITED KINGDOM Cont.
11. Consolidated financial statements	11. Consolidated accounts or consolidated financial statements (the term group accounts or group financial statements is also used, and this term includes consolidated accounts as well as other forms of group accounts)
12. Pooling of interests	12. Merger accounting
13. Purchase accounting	13. Acquisition accounting
14. Paid-in surplus (includes contributed capital and capitalised earnings)	14. Share premium (but excludes contributed capital and capitalised earnings)
15. Affiliated enterprise	15. Associated or related company

DIFFERENCES IN FINANCIAL STATEMENT FORMAT

The basic financial statements are generally the same in both countries, although the format, and sometimes the content, of the statements are different. They are as follows:

United States	United Kingdom
Balance sheet	Balance sheet
Income statement	Profit and loss account
Statement of cash flows	Statement of source and application of funds

Balance sheets prepared under US GAAP generally show assets and liabilities in decreasing order of liquidity (cash and notes payable being shown first), and the equity section appears after liabilities. Balance sheets prepared under UK practices generally show assets in the reverse order of liquidity.

US income statements are usually prepared in a format that shows all the elements used in determining net income (that is, sales, cost of sales, gross margin, operating expenses, income taxes, revenue and other expenses, extraordinary items, etc.). Under the Companies Act 1985, UK companies have the option of choosing a profit and loss account format which classifies expenses either by type or by function. If it improves clarity, the line-items may be shown in notes, rather than on the face of the statement. Certain items, however, such as interest, depreciation and amortisation, land rents received, and rental expense on plant and machinery must be disclosed regardless of the format adopted.

The US statement of cash flows classifies cash receipts and payments according to whether they stem from operating, investing or financing activities. Under US rules, a statement of cash flows is required for all profit-orientated business entities whenever both a balance sheet and an income statement are presented. Under UK rules, a statement of source and application of funds is required for all enterprises (except those with turnover or gross income less than £25,000 per annum) whose financial statements are intended to give a true and fair view of the financial position and profit or loss. The UK statement generally begins with pre-tax profit or loss, whereas the US statement begins with net income or loss on an after-tax basis.

As noted earlier, the Companies Act 1985 incorporates the accounting requirements of the EC Fourth Directive that governs the annual accounts of individual companies. There are two balance sheet formats and four profit and loss account formats permitted under the Act. Each format provides for specific headings and sub-headings, and these are required to be shown in a fixed order. Once a company selects a format it cannot change that format unless it can justify the change and also discloses that justification in the notes to the financial statements. The new Companies Act contains a schedule that details a form and content of consolidated financial statements.

Although the Companies Act provides that companies should follow specific formats and many other rules, it nonetheless contains the overriding requirement that the financial statements must give a true and fair view. If following these rules and formats would not result in the accounts giving a true and fair view, the company must depart from them to the extent necessary, and disclose the particulars, reasons and effect.

CHAPTER THREE

DIFFERENCES IN SPECIFIC

ACCOUNTING PRACTICES

— GENERAL

UNITED STATES

3.1 BASIS OF ACCOUNTING

Financial statements are generally prepared on the basis of historical cost. Exceptions are made to this general rule when the historical cost of an asset appears to have been impaired (for example, the lower of cost or market basis for valuation of inventories). Information about current values that exceed historical cost, if presented at all, is presented in the form of supplemental disclosures.

UNITED KINGDOM

3.1 BASIS OF ACCOUNTING

Although historical cost is the usual basis of accounting, this basis is often modified by the revaluation of land and buildings and of investments. Net surpluses arising from revaluations should be recorded as a credit to non-distributable reserves and not as part of profit (net income) for the year or distributable reserves (retained earnings). The Companies Act 1985 requires that surpluses and deficits arising from revaluations be recorded in revaluation reserves. If, on revaluation of an asset, a deficit arises that exceeds a previous surplus on that asset, then the excess should be charged to the profit and loss account. By law, a company must make provision if any fixed asset has diminished in value and this reduction is expected to be permanent.

The Companies Act 1985 permits current cost financial statements as the primary financial statements.

UNITED STATES

3.2 CHANGES IN ACCOUNTING PRINCIPLES/POLICIES

APBO 20 (AO6)

The cumulative effect, based on a retroactive computation, of a change from one generally accepted principle to another should be reported as a separate item in determining net income in the period of change (with three specific exceptions). Prior-year financial statements should not be restated. However, restated income before extraordinary items and net income on a pro forma basis should be shown on the face of the income statement for each prior period presented.

However, FASB pronouncements set out the manner of adopting any new accounting principle from those accepted previously. Many of them require restatement of prior-year financial statements, rather than the method generally required by APB Opinion 20.

A change to the declining balance method of calculating depreciation from another method, for example, should be treated as a change in accounting principle. The cumulative effect of such a change should be reported separately in earnings as described above. A change in estimated useful life or residual value, however, (if it is not a correction of an error) is a change in an accounting estimate, and should be accounted for prospectively.

UNITED KINGDOM

3.2   CHANGES IN ACCOUNTING PRINCIPLES/POLICIES

SSAP 6 (Revised)
Material cumulative effects of changes in accounting policies should
be treated as prior-period adjustments (see item 3.11 on page 39).
The results and the balance sheets of any prior periods presented
should be restated to reflect the results and the state of affairs that
would have been shown if the new policy had been adopted in the
earlier period. Where practicable, the effect of the change on the
results for the preceding year should be disclosed separately.

SSAP 12 (Revised)
A change from one method of calculating depreciation to another
method is not a change of accounting policy, and should be accounted
for prospectively. The effect of a change, if material, should be
disclosed in the year of change. The cumulative effect of a change
in estimated asset lives should, if future results would be materially
distorted by the change, be reported in the profit and loss account
in the year of change.

UNITED STATES

3.3 BUSINESS COMBINATIONS

A. General

APBO 16 (B 50)

Business combinations are accounted for as either purchases or poolings of interests. However, these two methods are not alternatives for the same business combination. If the combination satisfies each condition that is specified in APB 16 (including basically share for share exchange), then the pooling of interests method must be used. Otherwise, the purchase method applies.

B. Acquisition date

APBO 16 (B 50)

The date of acquisition of a company is normally the date on which effective control of the acquired company is transferred to the acquiring company. For convenience, a date at the end of an accounting period between the initiation date and the consummation date may often be so designated.

C. Applying the pooling/purchase methods

APBO 16, FAS 96 (B 50)

Under the pooling of interests method, the financial statements of the combined company are restated to show the previously separate companies as if they had always been combined. No adjustments are made to the amounts previously included in the separate financial statements.

Under the purchase method, the acquired company's assets and liabilities are adjusted to reflect fair values, and goodwill is

UNITED KINGDOM

3.3 BUSINESS COMBINATIONS

A. General

SSAP 23

If a business combination satisfies all of the merger conditions in the standard, then the group may use either merger accounting or acquisition accounting to account for the business combination. If the business combination fails to satisfy any of the merger conditions, then the group must use acquisition accounting.

A fundamental review of accounting for mergers and acquisitions is currently being undertaken by the ASC, which is likely to result in major changes to existing accounting practice.

B. Acquisition date

SSAP 14

The date of acquisition of an acquired company is normally determined as being the earlier of the date on which the offer becomes or is declared unconditional, and the date on which the purchase consideration passes. This applies even if the purchaser has a right to share in the profits of the acquired business from an earlier date.

C. Applying the pooling/purchase methods

SSAP 23

SSAP 23 states that under merger accounting, the financial statements of the combined group are restated to show the previously separate companies as if they had always been combined. No adjustments are made to the amounts previously included in the separate financial statements, except for any adjustments that are needed to achieve uniform accounting policies throughout the group.

UNITED STATES

recognised as appropriate, based on the purchase price paid. Under APBO 11, deferred income tax accounts of the acquired company should not be recorded by the purchaser because they do not represent timing differences under US GAAP. Instead, the tax bases of assets and liabilities acquired are considered in the determination of fair values. FAS 96, whose effective date is not yet mandatory, alters this treatment. The new requirement states that the tax basis of an asset or liability shall not be a factor in determining its fair value. Any deferred tax assets or liabilities related to specific assets or liabilities acquired should be accounted for separately (see item 4.12 on page 70).

The financial statements of the companies are combined as at the acquisition date. They are not restated to include the results of the operations of the acquired company for periods prior to the acquisition. However, for public enterprises pro forma results of operations should be disclosed in a note for the immediately preceding period as though the companies had been combined at the beginning of that period.

Fair value adjustments determined on the basis of the purchase transaction are recognised in the combined financial statements, but they are not necessarily recognised in the separate financial statements of the acquired company.

D. Goodwill

APBO 17 (I 60), APBO 16 (B 50)

Goodwill arising on a purchase should be amortised over the useful life of the goodwill, but the period should not exceed 40 years. Amortisation of goodwill acquired before 1 November 1970 is not required unless a permanent impairment has occurred. In that case, the amount of goodwill impaired should be written down immediately.

SSAP 14, SSAP 22 (Revised), SSAP 23

In acquisition accounting, fair values should be attributed to assets and liabilities acquired (including deferred taxation). In practice, certain assets such as stocks and plant and machinery are not always adjusted. A discussion paper 'Fair value in the context of acquisition accounting' was issued by the ASC in June 1988. It addresses the practical problems of applying fair values to assets and liabilities in a comprehensive manner and makes recommendations.

In acquisition accounting, the results of the acquired company should be brought into the group accounts from the date of acquisition only.

Consolidated financial statements of groups with material acquisitions should contain sufficient information about the results of the subsidiaries acquired to enable the shareholders to appreciate the effect those results have on the consolidated results. SSAP 22 (Revised), issued in July 1989, contains additional disclosure requirements relating to fair value adjustments and goodwill, in respect of material acquisitions.

Fair value adjustments are recognised in the consolidated financial statements. Also, they are often used as a basis for revaluing certain assets in the separate financial statements of the acquired company, but there is no requirement to do so.

D. Goodwill

SSAP 22

Purchased goodwill should normally be written off against reserves immediately on acquisition. However, it may be carried as an asset and amortised over its useful economic life. SSAP 22 does not specify a maximum period for amortisation.

UNITED STATES

'Negative goodwill' (namely, that arising where the total of the fair values of the individual assets and liabilities exceed the overall purchase price) is accounted for by pro rata allocation against the fair values of property and other non-monetary assets. If the allocation reduces such non-monetary assets to zero value, the remainder of the excess over cost is classified as a deferred credit and amortised systematically to income over the estimated period of benefit but not in excess of 40 years.

UNITED KINGDOM

Negative goodwill should be credited directly to reserves.

UNITED STATES

3.4 CONSOLIDATED FINANCIAL STATEMENTS

ARB 43, ARB 51, FAS 94 (C 51)

A. Comparability of periods included

Financial statements of subsidiaries with periods that are different by not more than about three months are generally acceptable for consolidation. Abnormal transactions in intervening periods should be disclosed or otherwise recognised as appropriate.

B. Companies included in consolidated financial statements

The consolidation should include only those subsidiaries over which the company has effective control which is other than temporary. The US now requires consolidation of a majority-owned subsidiary even if it has 'non-homogeneous' operations (e.g., finance subsidiary of a manufacturing concern).

UNITED KINGDOM

3.4 CONSOLIDATED FINANCIAL STATEMENTS

SSAP 14

A. Comparability of periods included

Financial statements of all subsidiaries in the consolidation should wherever practicable be prepared for the same period. This may require the use of specially-prepared financial statements for those subsidiaries that have different financial year ends. If different periods are unavoidable, the reason for using the different dates should be disclosed. Adjustments are required to the consolidated financial statements for any abnormal transactions in the intervening period. The Companies Act 1989 contains provisions that will make the UK treatment similar to the US, by only permitting consolidation of financial statements of subsidiaries with year ends not earlier than three months before that of the parent.

B. Companies included in consolidated financial statements

The rules are similar to the US except that subsidiaries in businesses completely dissimilar (non-homogeneous) to that of the rest of the group should be excluded from consolidation and stated on an equity basis. The Companies Act 1989, however, contains provisions which are likely to restrict the exemption from consolidation to banking and insurance subsidiaries where these activities are different from the rest of the group.

The Companies Act 1985 contains a legal definition of a subsidiary. This has led to the creation of some very complex group structures to create what are commonly known as controlled non-subsidiaries, which are not consolidated. However, the Companies Act 1989, together with an Exposure Draft issued by the ASC, contain provisions which will radically widen the definition of a subsidiary for the purposes of consolidation.

UNITED STATES

3.5 FOREIGN CURRENCY TRANSLATION

A. Functional currency

FAS 52 (F 60)

An entity's 'functional currency' is defined as the primary currency in which an entity operates and generates cash flows. It may be the currency of the country in which it operates (for companies whose operations are relatively independent and self-contained within a country), or it may be the parent company's functional currency (for companies whose operations directly impact and are an extension of the operations of the parent company).

FAS 52 provides guidance on determining the functional currency, but it recognises that this matter requires management judgement. In most cases, the currency of the country in which the company operates (the local currency) would be designated as the functional currency.

B. Translation of foreign currency financial statements

Translation for purposes of consolidation, combination, or use of the equity method of accounting is performed as follows:

Translations of financial statements from the functional currency to the reporting currency are at current exchange rates (rates at the balance sheet date for assets and liabilities and weighted average rates for revenues and expenses). Translations of capital stock and other paid-in capital are at appropriate historical rates. Translation adjustments are accumulated as a separate component of equity until the liquidation of the investment.

Financial statements in a currency other than the entity's functional currency are first 're-measured' in the functional currency. This re-measurement process is performed basically by applying the temporal method. Exchange gains and losses are taken into income currently.

UNITED KINGDOM

3.5 FOREIGN CURRENCY TRANSLATION

A. Functional currency

SSAP 20

The same concept of 'functional currency' is used, although not referred to as such. The currency of the country in which the company operates (the local currency) would probably be identified as the functional currency in virtually all cases.

B. Translation of foreign currency financial statements

The same principles broadly apply as in the US. However, amounts in the profit and loss account may be translated using either an average rate method or the exchange rate in effect at the balance sheet date, provided there is consistency of treatment from one period to the next. Translation differences are recorded as adjustments to reserves. However, there is no requirement for such adjustments to be accumulated separately.

Financial statements in currencies of countries in highly inflationary economies should be adjusted, where possible to reflect current price levels before translating to the reporting currency. A 'highly inflationary economy' is not defined in the UK.

UNITED STATES

Financial statements in currencies of countries in highly inflationary economies (100% or greater inflation in a three-year period) are translated (that is 're-measured') using the temporal method.

C. Foreign currency transactions

Foreign currency transactions are translated to the entity's functional currency using the exchange rates in effect on the dates of the transactions. Assets and liabilities are subsequently adjusted to balance sheet rates, and gains and losses are taken to income currently. Specific rules apply for gains and losses on forward exchange contracts.

Gains and losses on transactions that are either designated hedges of net foreign investments or long-term inter-company investment transactions are deferred and included directly in the separate equity component referred to above.

C. Foreign currency transactions

Generally the same method applies as in the US, except that average rates for a period may be used as an approximation instead of historical rates. Some translation gains and losses would be treated as extraordinary if the underlying transactions were also treated as extraordinary. The UK standard does not deal with forward exchange contracts except to allow foreign currency assets and liabilities to be translated at contracted rates, instead of the rate at the balance sheet date.

Exchange gains or losses on foreign currency borrowings that have been used to finance, or provide a hedge against, foreign equity investments may be offset as reserve movements against the exchange differences arising on the retranslation of the net investments. The offset is restricted to the amount of exchange differences arising on the net investments. In addition, such borrowings should not exceed the amount of cash that the net investments are expected to generate, whether from profits or otherwise.

UNITED STATES

3.6 NON-MONETARY TRANSACTIONS

APBO 29 (N 35)
Accounting for non-monetary transactions (that is, those transactions involving only assets or liabilities whose amounts are not fixed in terms of any unit of currency) should generally be based on the fair value of the assets or the services involved. Gains and losses on exchanges of non-monetary assets should be recognised in these cases.

3.7 SEGMENT REPORTING

FAS 14, 18, 21, 24, 30 (S 20)
The financial statements of public companies should include disaggregated information about the enterprise's operations in different industries, its foreign operations and export sales, and its major customers. For each reportable segment and for foreign operations an enterprise should present information about:

● Sales to unaffiliated customers and sales or transfers to other industry segments of the enterprise.

● Operating profit or loss.

● The aggregate carrying amount of identifiable assets.

● Other related disclosures.

Depreciation expense and capital expenditures are also required to be disclosed for each reportable segment.

UNITED KINGDOM

3.6 NON-MONETARY TRANSACTIONS

No specific requirements for non-monetary transactions have been established. Individual transactions are handled in various ways, depending on their merits (namely, some at fair value, some at historical cost; certain exchanges of services may not be recognised at all).

3.7 SEGMENT REPORTING

The Companies Act 1985 requires companies to provide in the notes to their financial statements a geographical analysis of turnover, together with an analysis of turnover and profit before tax by class of business. This information need not be disclosed, though, if the directors consider it would be seriously prejudicial to the interests of the company. However, the International Stock Exchange's Continuing Obligations requires quoted companies to provide a geographical analysis of both turnover and contribution to trading results of those trading operations carried on by the company outside the UK and the Republic of Ireland.

The ASC issued ED 45 'Segmental Reporting' in November 1988 which proposes to expand the disclosure requirements for segmental information in the financial statements of all public and large companies.

UNITED STATES

3.8 RELATED PARTY TRANSACTIONS

FAS 57 (R 36)

In general, accounting for transactions with related parties is the same as accounting for transactions with unrelated parties. An exception is made in instances where the related party relationship has affected the substance of the transaction.

Transactions with related parties, if material, must be disclosed in the financial statements. Such disclosures should include:

- The nature of relationship involved.
- A description of the transactions, including those to which nominal or no amounts were ascribed.
- Amounts of transactions and balances included in the financial statements, and the effects of any change in establishing terms from that used in the preceding period.

Any representations about related party transactions being carried out on an arm's-length basis must be substantiated. Under certain circumstances common ownership or management control should be disclosed even though there may be no transactions between the related enterprises.

3.8 RELATED PARTY TRANSACTIONS

There is no general requirement for disclosing transactions with related parties, although there are specific requirements in the Companies Act 1985 and the International Stock Exchange's Continuing Obligations that capture the majority of related party transactions that would be reported in the US.

The ASC issued ED 46 'Disclosure of Related Party Transactions' in July 1989 which contains proposals for disclosure of abnormal transactions with related parties and disclosure of the existence and nature of controlling related party relationships.

These cover in particular transactions with directors, and disclosures relating to substantial shareholders, group companies and related companies.

UNITED STATES

3.9 ENTERPRISES THAT ARE IN THE DEVELOPMENT STAGE

FAS 7 (De 4)

The financial statements of enterprises that are in the development stage should incorporate the same accounting policies as those of any other profit-making organisation, including those relating to the recoverability of deferred costs. The following additional information must be disclosed relating to the development activities during the entire period to date of the development stage:

- Accumulated net losses and deficits during the development stage.
- A cumulative income statement showing total revenues, expenses, etc. during the development stage.
- Cumulative cash inflows and cash outflows during the development stage.
- Certain detailed information on shareholders' transactions.

UNITED KINGDOM

3.9 ENTERPRISES THAT ARE IN THE DEVELOPMENT STAGE

No additional disclosures are required or normally made for such entities.

UNITED STATES

3.10 INTERIM FINANCIAL STATEMENTS

APBO 28 (I 73)
In general, the results for each interim period should be based on the accounting practices used in preparing the annual financial statements. Certain practices, however, require modification for interim purposes. This pronouncement contains specific guidance for preparing interim statements. SEC companies must report quarterly.

3.11 PRIOR-PERIOD ADJUSTMENTS

APBO 9 and 20, FAS 16 (A 35)
Prior-period adjustments are limited to the following items:
- Corrections of errors in financial statements of prior periods.
- Adjustments resulting from the realisation of the taxation benefits of pre-acquisition operating loss carry-forwards of purchased subsidiaries (for entities reporting under APBO 11).

UNITED KINGDOM

3.10 INTERIM FINANCIAL STATEMENTS

The form and content of interim financial statements are not covered by SSAPs. The International Stock Exchange's Continuing Obligations require half-yearly profits statements for listed companies.

3.11 PRIOR-PERIOD ADJUSTMENTS

SSAP 6 (Revised)
Prior-period adjustments are limited to the following items, where material:

- Corrections of fundamental errors in financial statements of prior periods.
- Changes in accounting policies (see item 3.2 on page 19).

CHAPTER FOUR

DIFFERENCES IN SPECIFIC

ACCOUNTING PRACTICES

— REVENUE AND EXPENSE

UNITED STATES

4.1 REVENUE RECOGNITION

A. Revenue recognition when a right of return by the buyer exists

FAS 48 (R 75)

Revenue can be recognised only if all of the following conditions are met:

- Selling price is fixed or determinable and does not depend upon resale.
- The buyer has independent economic substance, and his obligation is unchanged by theft, damage, etc. of the product.
- Future returns can be estimated and are accrued.

If any of the conditions are not met, the transaction is treated as a consignment of inventory, and it is not recorded as a sale.

B. Product financing arrangements

FAS 49 (D 18)

Product financing arrangements generally involve the sale of a product together with a related commitment either to repurchase the product or to purchase either a similar product or one of which the product is a component, etc. in the future.

The sponsor (that is, the seller of the product) should not recognise the transaction as a sale. Instead, both parties should recognise the transaction for what it is — a financing arrangement.

C. Sales of real estate

FAS 66, 67, 98 (R 10)

For sales of real estate, other than retail land sales, there are specific criteria for profit recognition by the full accrual and several other deferral methods, depending on whether a sale has been consummated, the extent of the buyer's investment in the property being sold, whether the seller's receivable is subject to future

UNITED KINGDOM

4.1. REVENUE RECOGNITION

A. Revenue recognition when a right of return by the buyer exists

This is not specifically covered by any accounting pronouncements. Outright consignment arrangements are accounted for in a manner similar to that under US rules.

B. Product financing arrangements

These are not covered by any existing accounting standards. However, ED 42 'Accounting for Special Purpose Transactions', issued by the ASC in March 1988, deals with sale and repurchase agreements and proposes they should be accounted for as financing arrangements rather than sales in certain circumstances.

C. Sales of real estate

SSAP 21

This is not specifically covered by any accounting pronouncement in the UK. Generally profit is recognised, and the sale treated as realised, either when legal title passes or when there is an unconditional exchange of contract. Where unusual terms are included in the sale agreement, the accounting position will generally

UNITED STATES

subordination, and the degree of the seller's continuing involvement with the property after sale. Different criteria for profit recognition are applied to sales in retail land sales projects.

Where the transaction involves a sale-leaseback, any profit or loss on the sale is deferred and amortised in proportion to the amortisation of the leased asset if a finance lease or in proportion to the rental expense, if an operating lease.

UNITED KINGDOM

follow the legal position with full disclosure of any unusual terms being noted in the financial statements. However, ED42 would require the substance of the transaction to be followed in some circumstances.

In a sale and leaseback transaction that results in a finance lease, any profit or loss is deferred and amortised over the shorter of the lease term and the useful life of the asset. In an operating leaseback, if the sale is at fair value, any profit or loss should be recognised immediately; otherwise deferral may be required.

UNITED STATES

4.2 LEASE TRANSACTIONS

FAS 13, 17, 22, 23, 26, 27, 28, 29, 91 and 98 (L 10)

Those lease transactions that meet any of four criteria are required to be treated as capital leases, that is capitalised in the financial statements of the lessee (the user of the asset) and treated as either a sales-type or direct financing lease (depending on the circumstances) by the lessor (the legal owner of the asset). The four criteria for identifying capital leases are summarised generally as follows:

- The lease transfers ownership to the lessee.
- The lease contains a bargain purchase option.
- The lease term (including bargain renewal periods) covers 75% or more of the remaining economic life of the asset (with exceptions for certain used property).
- The present value of the minimum lease payments (including termination penalties, etc.) is 90% or more of the asset's fair value.

Each of the terms used has a specific meaning within the pronouncements. Leases not meeting any of the four criteria are classified as operating leases.

The manner in which income or expense is recognised and presented, and the disclosures required, which include long-term lease obligation information, are also stipulated in the pronouncements. There are rules for classifying leases involving real estate, under the criteria referred to above, as well as rules relating to terminations and renewals.

The manner in which lessors determine the dealer's or the manufacturer's profit from sales-type leases is set out. So is the manner in which income from direct financing leases is recognised. Lessors must account for initial direct costs as part of the investment

UNITED KINGDOM

4.2 LEASE TRANSACTIONS

SSAP 21

SSAP 21 is based on the same concepts as FAS 13, but its provisions are far less complex. It also has a number of important differences from FAS 13. The way in which leases are classified is simpler and more subjective than FAS 13, and the way in which lessees disclose information about their commitments under finance and operating leases is different from that required by FAS 13. Also, the method of income recognition that lessors use for accounting for finance leases is fundamentally different from that of FAS 13.

Those leases that transfer substantially all the risks and rewards of ownership to the lessee (finance leases) are capitalised in the accounts of the lessee (the user of the asset) and treated as a receivable in the accounts of the lessor. Under all other leases (operating leases) the rentals are expensed in the accounts of the lessee, and the assets are treated as fixed assets in the accounts of the lessor.

A lease is presumed to transfer substantially all the risks and rewards of ownership to the lessee if the present value of the minimum lease payments amounts to substantially all (normally 90% or more) of the leased asset's fair value. However, this presumption can be rebutted in exceptional circumstances if it can be clearly demonstrated that the lease in question does not transfer substantially all the risks and rewards of ownership to the lessee. Conversely, leases that do not satisfy the 90% test may still be classified as finance leases, depending on a subjective assessment of where the risks and rewards lie.

The disclosure requirement for the maturity of finance lease obligations is similar to that required for loans under the Companies Act, and the obligation is usually disclosed net of future interest.

UNITED STATES

in the lease. Except for three-party leveraged leases, the method of income recognition does not take the timing of accelerated income tax benefits into account. US rules do not permit the 'investment period method' of income recognition (the method common in the UK) whereby income is allocated over only the initial period in which the lessor has a positive net of tax investment in the transaction.

UNITED KINGDOM

Commitments under operating leases are disclosed in terms of the annual rental level expected for the following one year period, analysed by lease expiry date, rather than the aggregate lease obligation as required under FAS 13. There are no special rules for classifying leases of real estate or rules for dealing with terminations and renewals.

Lessors are required to recognise the gross earnings from finance leases on a constant rate of return basis based on their net of tax investment in the lease. The investment period method is widely used by leasing companies in the UK.

UNITED STATES

4.3 EXTRAORDINARY ITEMS

APBO 9 and 30, FAS 4 (I 17)

Extraordinary items are those transactions that are distinguished by their *unusual* nature and the *infrequency* of their occurrence, considering the environment in which the entity operates.

   Although the stated criteria for extraordinary items in the two countries are similar, and although such items are similarly segregated, net of tax, from ordinary operations, the US application of the criteria is much more restrictive. The term 'infrequent' is more narrowly defined in the US pronouncements to mean 'not reasonably expected to recur in the foreseeable future'. Conversely, however, material gains and losses from the extinguishing of debt (item 4.4 on page 52), tax benefits of net operating loss carry-forwards (item 4.12.B on page 72) and the net effect of adjustments required when an enterprise discontinues operating as a regulated entity (see FAS 101) are specifically required by US pronouncements to be treated as extraordinary items.

UNITED KINGDOM

4.3 EXTRAORDINARY ITEMS

SSAP 6 (Revised)

Extraordinary items are those that derive from events or transactions that fall outside the ordinary activities of the business, that are material, and are not expected to recur either frequently or regularly. Examples of items that could be extraordinary (excluded from the results of ordinary activities) and exceptional (included in the results of ordinary activities) are given in the standard.

UNITED STATES

4.4 REPORTING GAINS AND LOSSES ON THE EXTINGUISHMENT OF DEBT

APBO 26 and FAS 4, 64, 76, 84 (D 14)

Differences between the reacquisition price and the net carrying amount of debt extinguished prior to maturity should be recognised as gains or losses and included in income currently. Material aggregate gains or losses recognised when long-term debt is extinguished (except those from cash purchases of debt made to satisfy sinking fund requirements), including troubled debt restructurings, should be classified as extraordinary items and reported net of the related income tax effect. (See item 5.11 on page 102 as to the limitations with respect to troubled debt restructurings.)

Under certain circumstances the same early extinguishment rules can be applied to 'in-substance' debt defeasances whereby a debtor irrevocably places cash or other 'essentially risk free' assets in a trust to be used solely for satisfying principal and interest payments on a specific fixed rate obligation. Provided that the possibility that the debtor will be required to make future payments with respect to that debt is remote, the debt is considered extinguished.

The above rules do not apply to conversions of convertible debt in instances involving a change in the original conversion terms, or payment of additional consideration, in order to induce conversion of the debt to equity securities. The cost of such an inducement offer must be recognised as an expense and may not be classified as an extraordinary item.

UNITED KINGDOM

4.4 REPORTING GAINS AND LOSSES ON THE EXTINGUISHMENT OF DEBT

Gains and losses of this type are not referred to specifically in existing SSAPs. Whether such items are recognised in income currently and, if so, whether they are treated as extraordinary, depends upon the circumstances relating to the transaction. SSAP 6 (Revised) provides that a gain or loss would be treated as extraordinary only if it is regarded as being outside the ordinary activities of the business, is material, and is not expected to recur either frequently or regularly.

There is no comparable practice in UK accounting for 'in-substance' debt defeasance. The Companies Act 1985 generally prohibits the offset of assets against liabilities unless such offset is legally enforceable. Offset is therefore unlikely to be permitted if a debtor has not been released from the primary obligation.

UK accounting does not specifically deal with induced conversions of convertible debt. In practice the cost of an inducement offer is not measured and, thus, is only reflected in shareholders' equity upon conversion.

UNITED STATES

4.5 DISPOSALS OF SUBSIDIARIES, OPERATIONS, ETC.

APBO 30 (I 13)

A. General requirements

Discontinued operations of business segments are required to be reported separately from continuing operations. These include:

- Results of operations for the current year and restatement of prior years for segments that have been, or will be, disposed of, plus
- Gains or losses on such disposals, including estimated amounts.

Discontinued operations should be identified as 'discontinued operations', and they should be reported net of related tax effects, separately from income from continuing operations.

'Business segment' is narrowly defined. Disposals of those operations that do not meet this criterion cannot be accounted for as described above.

B. Measurement and disposal dates

The measurement date for the purposes of determining the gain or loss on the disposition of a business segment is the date on which management commits itself to a formal plan of action (regardless of whether a buyer has been found), and gains and losses should

UNITED KINGDOM

4.5 DISPOSALS OF SUBSIDIARIES, OPERATIONS, ETC.

SSAP 14, SSAP 6 (Revised)

A. General requirements

Where subsidiaries are sold, the consolidated profit and loss account should include their results up to the date of disposal. Gains or losses on disposals would normally be treated as extraordinary items. In the consolidated profit and loss account sufficient information should be given to enable shareholders to appreciate the effect of those disposals on the consolidated results. There is no restatement of prior year's results.

In the case of closure of a business segment, provision should be made for the consequence of all decisions taken up to the balance sheet date, including debits and credits arising from trading after commencing the implementation of the closure. Profits or losses from terminated activities arising from trading before the commencement of implementation are part of the ordinary trading results, but may require separate disclosure to enable the results of continued operations to be ascertained. Profits or losses arising from the discontinuance of a business segment, either through termination or disposal, are disclosed as extraordinary items.

As in the US, 'business segment' is narrowly defined but is in practice given a broader interpretation in the UK. The discontinuance of activities that do not qualify should be dealt with in arriving at profit or loss on ordinary activities.

B. Measurement and disposal dates

The date of disposal of a subsidiary is normally determined to be the earlier of the date on which the sale offer becomes, or is declared, unconditional, and the date on which the sale consideration passes. This requires a buyer before any gain or loss on the disposal can

UNITED STATES

be first recognised based on this date. The disposal date is the date on which a sale is closed, or, if the disposal is by abandonment, the date on which operations actually cease.

UNITED KINGDOM

be recognised. However, SSAP 17 (Accounting for Post Balance Sheet Events) and the Companies Act 1985 would generally require current recognition of any permanent decline in value. The implementation date in the context of terminated activities is not defined, but is generally taken as the date from which management takes action to carry out a decision to close down a business segment.

UNITED STATES

4.6 IMPUTING INTEREST ON RECEIVABLES AND PAYABLES

APBO 21 (I 69)

The substance of transactions involving receivables or payables should rule over the form of those transactions. Accordingly, in certain circumstances when the rate of interest relating to those transactions is not a fair rate of interest, additional interest should be imputed on receivables and payables. (These requirements do not apply to certain debts such as short-term amounts incurred in the normal course of trade.)

Assets acquired by incurring liabilities are recorded at historical cost, measured by the *present value* of the amounts to be paid.

4.7 ACCOUNTING FOR NON-REFUNDABLE LENDING FEES

FAS 91

Loan origination fees and certain other origination costs must be recognised over the life of the related loan as an adjustment of yield. Loan commitment fees should be deferred except for certain retrospectively determined fees.

UNITED KINGDOM

4.6 IMPUTING INTEREST ON RECEIVABLES AND PAYABLES

There is no requirement to discount receivables and payables. Generally, the imputation of interest is rare.

The cost of assets acquired by incurring liabilities would normally be measured by the *face value* of the liabilities incurred.

4.7 ACCOUNTING FOR NON-REFUNDABLE LENDING FEES

These are not specifically covered by accounting pronouncements in the UK.

UNITED STATES

4.8   ACCOUNTING FOR PENSIONS

FAS 87 (P 16)

A.   Cost recognition

Net periodic pension cost is made up of several components that reflect different aspects of the employer's financial arrangements as well as the cost of benefits earned by employees, without regard to how the employer decides to finance the plan.

B.   Actuarial method

The pronouncement stipulates the use of the 'projected unit credit' method which uses the cost of securing benefits accruing each year for scheme members. Allowance is made for projected future salary increases.

C.   Pension cost

Pension cost is determined as the sum of:

- Service cost.
- Interest cost.
- Return on plan assets.
- Net amortisation and deferral.

D.   Actuarial assumptions

- Discount rates — rates at which the pension benefits could effectively be settled.

UNITED KINGDOM

4.8 ACCOUNTING FOR PENSIONS

SSAP 24

A. Cost recognition

The employer should recognise the expected cost of providing pensions on a systematic and rational basis over the period during which he derives benefit from the employees' services.

B. Actuarial method

The standard is flexible as regards the selection of actuarial methods for determining pension cost, provided that the method chosen fulfils certain criteria. In practice, many methods may be permissible.

C. Pension cost

Pension cost is determined as the sum of:

- Regular cost — this is defined as the consistent ongoing cost recognised under the actuarial method used. Regular cost should be a substantially level percentage of the current and expected future pensionable payroll in the light of the current actuarial assumptions.
- Variations from regular cost — these may arise, for example, from surpluses or deficiencies in the pension scheme that are caused by actual experience differing from the assumptions.

D. Actuarial assumptions

The standard does not specify assumptions. However, the actuarial assumptions and method, taken as a whole, should lead to the actuary's best estimate of the cost of providing the pension benefits promised.

UNITED STATES

- Rates of return on assets — rates that reflect the average rate of earnings expected on funds invested to provide for the benefits included in the projected benefit obligation.
- Rates of salary increases.

E.   Assets and liabilities

An asset (or liability) should be set up in the employer's balance sheet where the net periodic pension cost is less than (or exceeds) the amount the employer has contributed. Similarly, if the capitalised value of accrued benefits based on pensionable service to date and current salaries, the 'accumulated benefit obligation', exceeds the market value of assets, then a liability should be recognised.

F.   Prior service cost

The capital cost of a benefit improvement must be recognised in equal amounts over the future period of service for which an employee active at the date of the amendment is expected to receive benefits under the plan.

UNITED KINGDOM

E. Assets and liabilities

A prepayment or provision should be recognised where pension cost differs from contributions paid, but there is no requirement to recognise other liabilities in respect of the funded status of a scheme.

F. Prior service cost

Past service costs arising from benefit improvements should normally be written off over the remaining service lives of the current employees.

For increases to pensions in payment, if the actuarial assumptions take them into account, the cost will form part of regular cost and will be charged over the service lives of the employees.

If however, the assumptions do not make provision for such increases, their capital cost,to the extent that it is not covered by a surplus in the scheme, should be expensed in the period of amendment.

UNITED STATES

4.9 ACCOUNTING FOR DEFERRED COMPENSATION COSTS — OTHER THAN PENSIONS

A. Deferred compensation contracts

APBO 12 (C 38)

The estimated present value of the future payments to be made under deferred compensation contracts should be accrued, over the period of active employment from the time the contract is entered into.

B. Compensated absences

FAS 43 (C 44)

This pronouncement relates primarily to vacation and holiday absences, but it may also include other absences. Employers must accrue liabilities for future absences if the compensation is for services already rendered and the rights to benefit either 'vest' (become unconditional) or 'accumulate'. No accrual is required for non-vesting sick pay benefits.

C. Special termination benefits

FAS 88 (P 16)

Where a company offers special termination benefits for a short period of time to its employees, a liability and a loss shall be recognised when the amount can be reasonably estimated and the employee accepts the offer. The benefits provided may include lump sum payments, periodic future payments, or both and should be accounted for at present values.

D. Disclosure of post-retirement health care and life insurance benefits

FAS 81 (P 50)

An employer that provides health care or life assurance benefits to retirees, their dependents, or survivors is required to disclose, at a minimum, the following information:

64

UNITED KINGDOM

4.9 ACCOUNTING FOR DEFERRED COMPENSATION COSTS — OTHER THAN PENSIONS

A. Deferred compensation contracts

No standard accounting policy presently exists.

B. Compensated absences

Holiday absences (including 'vacations' in US terminology, as well as bank holidays) are not specifically covered by any accounting pronouncement. Actual practice varies from accruals to cash basis.

C. Special termination benefits

SSAP 24

The statement applies to the granting of ex gratia pensions and in principle to the cost of providing other post-retirement benefits. The accounting treatment will depend on the nature of the benefit, but generally the cost would be recognised in full when the benefit is granted (discounted if appropriate) unless it is a benefit to be covered by a surplus in the employer's pension scheme.

D. Disclosure of post-retirement health care and life insurance benefits

These types of benefits are less prevalent in the UK than in the US.

UNITED STATES

- A description of the benefits provided and the employee groups covered.
- A description of the accounting and funding policies for the benefits.
- The cost of those benefits recognised in expense for the period.
- The effect of significant matters affecting the comparability of the cost recognised for all periods presented.

An Exposure Draft was issued in February 1989 which covers the accounting for post-retirement benefits other than pensions. This includes health care and life insurance. It recommends a change from the cash basis to an accruals basis. Hence, the cost of providing these benefits to employees, beneficiaries or dependents would be recognised over the employee's service period, similarly to accounting for pensions.

4.10 COMPENSATION AND SHARE OPTION AND SHARE PURCHASE PLANS

ARB 43, APBO 25 (C 47)
Specific criteria are established for identifying non-compensatory versus compensatory plans. Also specific rules are set out for determining fair values and for the timing and determination of compensation costs.

UNITED KINGDOM

There are no specific disclosure requirements and little is normally given, although SSAP 24, which primarily addresses pensions, may encourage more disclosure.

Although SSAP 24 applies in principle to accounting for the cost of other post-retirement benefits such as health care and life insurance, the ASC has issued a Technical Release which states that there is no obligation for companies to change from a cash basis to an accruals basis in respect of such benefits.

4.10 COMPENSATION AND SHARE OPTION AND SHARE PURCHASE PLANS

Such shares are normally accounted for as if the option prices represented the fair value of those shares. Therefore, no amounts are normally ascribed to compensation.

UNITED STATES

4.11 ACCOUNTING FOR RESEARCH AND DEVELOPMENT EXPENDITURE

FAS 2 (R 50)

All research and development expenditure as defined by the statement should be charged to expense when incurred. The amounts so charged should be disclosed separately.

The cost of materials and equipment or facilities that are acquired or constructed for research and development activities, and that have alternative future uses, should be capitalised as tangible assets when they are acquired or constructed. If they do not have alternative future uses, and therefore have no separate economic values, they should be charged to expense when they are incurred.

FAS 68 (R 55)

In situations involving research and development arrangements with outside parties, a determination must be made as to the extent that an obligation to repay the outside parties has been created. Such obligation is recorded as a liability and charged to research and development expense as incurred.

UNITED KINGDOM

4.11 ACCOUNTING FOR RESEARCH AND DEVELOPMENT EXPENDITURE

SSAP 13 (Revised)

Both SSAP 13 and the Companies Act 1985 distinguish between expenditure on 'research' and expenditure on 'development'. Expenditure on pure and applied research should be written off in the year in which it is incurred. Development expenditure should be written off in the year incurred except when certain specified criteria are satisfied. In such a case, it may be deferred to future periods and amortised by reference to either sales or the use of the product or process, or the period over which they are expected to be sold or used. Deferred development expenditure should be disclosed under intangible fixed assets in the balance sheet.

The cost of fixed assets acquired or constructed in order to provide facilities for research and development should be capitalised and depreciated over their useful life.

The total amount of research and development expenditure charged in the profit and loss account should be disclosed, distinguishing between the current year's expenditure and amounts amortised from deferred expenditure.

UNITED STATES

4.12 ACCOUNTING FOR DEFERRED TAXES
('TAXATION' IN THE UK)

FAS 96 was issued in December 1987. However, a number of preparers and users of financial statements expressed concern over the complexity of its application. As a consequence of these concerns, FAS 100 was issued in December 1988 postponing the implementation date of FAS 96 by an additional year. At present APBO 11 'Accounting for Income Taxes' and FAS 96 are in force. The FASB originally stated that it was not their intent to change FAS 96 but only to delay its implementation. It now appears that the FASB is considering changes to FAS 96 in response to significant criticism of the pronouncement.

A. General

APBO 11 (I 24)

Deferred taxes should be provided for on all timing differences (short term or long term). The calculation of such deferred taxes should be based on the 'deferred' (or 'deferral' in the UK) method.

The deferred method may be calculated using either the 'Gross Change' or 'Net Change' method provided it is consistently applied to all timing differences of a similar nature.

The nature of the timing differences on which the deferred taxes are based should be disclosed.

FAS 96

The FASB has reached these conclusions which are included in the standard:

- *Comprehensive Interperiod Tax Allocation.* A major conclusion of the FASB is that the concept established in APB Opinion No 11 of comprehensive interperiod tax allocation should continue to be required. Under this concept, tax effects are allocated to

70

UNITED KINGDOM

4.12 ACCOUNTING FOR DEFERRED TAXATION ('TAXES' IN THE US)

A. General

SSAP 15 (Revised)

Deferred tax should be computed under the liability method. Computation under the deferral method is prohibited. Deferred tax should only be accounted for on timing differences (short term and long term) to the extent that it is probable that a liability or asset will crystallise. It should not be accounted for to the extent that it is probable that a liability or asset will not crystallise.

The assessment of whether tax liabilities will or will not crystallise should be based on reasonable assumptions including financial plans or projections covering a period of years sufficient to enable an assessment to be made of the likely pattern of future tax liabilities.

A prudent view should be taken in the assessment of whether a tax liability will crystallise, particularly where financial plans are subject to uncertainty or not fully developed.

The amounts of deferred tax provided and unprovided, analysed by major components, should be disclosed by way of note. Deferred

UNITED STATES

the years when the related revenues or expenses are recognised in income for financial accounting purposes. The objective is matching. Income tax expense for a year includes the tax effects of all revenues and expenses recognised in determining pretax financial income for that year.

- *The Liability Method.* The FASB has concluded that the tax liability (or asset) approach to interperiod tax allocation should be used. Under the tax liability method, the tax effects of timing differences are determined using tax rates and tax laws expected to be in effect when the timing differences reverse. Unless future changes in rates or laws are known, those in effect at the date of the financial statements are used to initially calculate the tax effects. Balance sheet amounts are,however, adjusted for changes that occur or become known after the period of origination.

It should be noted that the US 'liability' method differs from the UK 'liability' method in that US deferred taxes are provided on all timing differences regardless of whether or not a liability is expected to 'crystallise'. Thus, the only similarity is that both methods require adjustment to balance sheet amounts when a change in tax rate after the period of origination is known or subsequently occurs. The new statement introduces the term 'temporary differences' as being differences between the tax basis of an asset or liability and its reported amount in the financial statements.

B. Net operating losses ('taxation losses' in the UK)
APBO 11 (I 24)
The tax benefit of net operating loss carry-forwards can be recognised when they arise only in the rare case where realisation of the benefit is assured beyond any reasonable doubt. Otherwise, the benefits are recognised only in the period they are actually realised and accounted for as an extraordinary item.

UNITED KINGDOM

tax provided in the current period should be shown separately as part of the tax charge.

B.   Taxation losses ('net operating losses' in the US)

The revised standard requires that deferred tax assets, including those arising from losses, should be recognised only when they are expected to be recoverable without replacement by equivalent debit balances. More detailed guidance on the circumstances where revenue and capital losses may be treated as recoverable is given

UNITED STATES

Loss carry-forward benefits can also be recognised when they arise by offsetting them against those existing net deferred tax credits that will reverse in the carry-forward period. Once these benefits are actually realised, however, they must be used first to reinstate the deferred tax credits offset previously.

FAS 96

The new standard only permits the recognition of a deferred tax asset for the tax benefit of net deductible amounts that could be realised by loss carryback from future years (1) to reduce a current deferred tax liability and (2) to reduce taxes paid in the current or a prior year.

Additionally, in business combinations, a deferred tax liability or asset shall be recognized in accordance with the requirements of the Statement for differences between the assigned values and the tax bases of the assets and liabilities recognized in a purchase business combination. If not recognized at the acquisition date, the tax benefits of an acquired operating loss or tax credit carry-forward for financial reporting that are recognized in financial statements after the acquisition date shall (a) first be applied to reduce to zero any goodwill and other non-current intangible assets related to the acquisition and(b) next be recognized as a reduction of income tax expense.

C. Deferred taxes on earnings of subsidiaries and affiliates
APBO 23 and 24 (I 42), FAS 96
Deferred taxes must be provided on undistributed earnings of minority-owned investee companies accounted for on the equity method. They must be provided as if such earnings will be transferred to the investor company or realised through sale of the equity investment.

UNITED KINGDOM

in an appendix to the standard. The realisation of loss carry-forward benefits is accounted for as part of the taxation charge on ordinary activities, and not as an extraordinary item.

Offsetting is also permitted under UK rules. However, deferred tax credits are not reinstated as long as there are sufficient remaining unrealised loss carry-forwards to cover them.

There are no specific rules as yet regarding the treatment of tax benefits in business combinations.

C. Deferred taxation of subsidiaries and affiliates

SSAP 15 (Revised)

Undistributed earnings of overseas subsidiaries or investments will create a timing difference only if there is an intention or obligation to remit them, and if remittance would result in a tax liability after taking account of any related double tax relief. In practice, provision for deferred taxation is rarely made.

UNITED STATES

The same requirements apply to undistributed earnings of subsidiaries. However, where there is sufficient evidence to show that the earnings of a subsidiary have been or will be indefinitely reinvested in that subsidiary , or that the earnings would be remitted only in a tax-free liquidation, deferred taxes should not be provided by the parent company on such unremitted earnings.

FAS 96 does not amend this approach.

D. Classification of deferred taxes

FAS 37 (I 28)

Deferred debits and credits (deferred taxation) related to an asset or a liability are classified as current or non-current based on the classification of the related asset or liability. Otherwise such classification is based on the expected reversal date of the related timing difference.

FAS 96

Under the new statement, the current amount shall be the net deferred tax consequence of temporary differences that will result in net taxable or deductible amounts during the next year. Deferred tax liabilities and assets attributable to different jurisdictions shall not be offset.

UNITED KINGDOM

D. Classification of deferred taxation

SSAP 15 (Revised)

Provision for deferred tax liabilities should be reduced by any deferred tax debit balances arising from separate categories of timing differences. The deferred tax balance should be disclosed under the balance sheet caption for 'provisions' and thus are classified as non-current.

UNITED STATES

4.13 ACCOUNTING FOR FUTURES CONTRACTS

FAS 80 (F 80)

A change in the market value of an open exchange-traded futures contract (other than contracts for foreign currencies) is recognised as a gain or loss in the period of the change unless the contract qualifies as a hedge of certain exposures to price or interest rate risk. Immediate gain or loss recognition is also required if the futures contract is intended to hedge an item that is reported at fair value.

If the specified hedge criteria are met, a change in the market value of the futures contract is either reported as an adjustment of the carrying amount of the hedged item or included in the measurement of a qualifying subsequent transaction.

UNITED KINGDOM

4.13 ACCOUNTING FOR FUTURES CONTRACTS

This is not specifically covered by any accounting pronouncement. Futures contracts are recorded in a number of ways including the treatment prescribed by FAS 80. A prime requirement is, however, full disclosure of the method of accounting used, especially where such contracts are treated as hedges.

UNITED STATES

4.14 EARNINGS PER SHARE (EPS)

APBO 15, FAS 21, 85 (E 09)

A. Applicability
If the company's securities (debt or equity) are publicly traded and if the company is not a wholly-owned subsidiary, EPS should be disclosed.

B. Presentation
EPS should be presented for income from continuing operations, income before extraordinary items, cumulative effect of a change in accounting principle and net income for all periods presented. It is recommended (but not required) that EPS amounts be presented for extraordinary items.

C. Primary vs fully diluted
The primary EPS amount should incorporate both the shares actually issued and stock options and other securities that are equivalent in substance to common stock (ordinary shares) and are also dilutive in their effect.

The fully diluted EPS amounts should reflect the dilutive effect that would occur if all other potentially dilutive securities were converted into common stock (ordinary shares).

D. Materiality of dilution
Securities with aggregate dilution of less than 3% need not be considered for either primary or fully diluted EPS calculations.

UNITED KINGDOM

4.14   EARNINGS PER SHARE (EPS)

SSAP 3

A. Applicability

EPS need be disclosed only if the company's equity shares are quoted on a recognised stock exchange. Also banking, insurance and certain other companies are exempted.

B. Presentation

EPS are normally stated only for profit before extraordinary items.

C. Primary vs fully diluted

The primary EPS amount is based on the equity shares actually issued and ranking for dividend in respect of the period. The fully diluted EPS reflects the dilutive effect of securities that may be converted into equity shares, options or warrants to subscribe for equity shares, and equity shares which will rank for dividend in a future period. (The fully diluted EPS should not be shown for the previous period reported unless the assumptions on which it was based still apply.)

D. Materiality of dilution

Fully diluted earnings per share need not be given unless the aggregate dilution is at least 5% of primary earnings per share.

CHAPTER FIVE

DIFFERENCES IN SPECIFIC

ACCOUNTING PRACTICES

— ASSETS, LIABILITIES

AND CAPITAL

UNITED STATES

5.1 CLASSIFICATION OF RECEIVABLES DUE AFTER MORE THAN ONE YEAR

ARB 43 (B 05)

Receivables due after more than one year must be excluded from current assets, except for certain specialised industries with longer operating cycles. Any receivables which, although currently due, are not expected to be collected within 12 months should also be excluded from current assets.

5.2 RECEIVABLES TRANSFERRED WITH RECOURSE

FAS 77 (R 20)

A transferor ordinarily should report a sale of receivables with recourse transaction as a sale if:

- the transferor surrenders its control of the future economic benefits relating to the receivables;
- the transferor can reasonably estimate its obligation under the recourse provisions; and
- the transferee cannot return the receivables to the transferor except pursuant to the recourse provisions.

If the above conditions are not met, the amount of proceeds from the transfer should be reported as a liability.

UNITED KINGDOM

5.1 CLASSIFICATION OF RECEIVABLES DUE AFTER MORE THAN ONE YEAR

The Companies Act 1985 requires all receivables to be included under current assets with footnote disclosure of amounts due after more than 12 months. In practice exceptions are sometimes made for material long-term receivables which may require separate non-current classification in order to present a 'true and fair view'.

5.2 RECEIVABLES TRANSFERRED WITH RECOURSE

This is not covered by any accounting pronouncement in the UK. The most frequent example of such a transaction in the UK results from the factoring of debts, where the treatment as required in FAS 77 would accord with best UK practice. The ASC are currently developing proposals for this subject which will be covered in a future accounting standard.

UNITED STATES

5.3 INVENTORY ('STOCKS' IN THE UK)

A. Cost methods

ARB 43 (I 78)

Inventory is normally stated at the lower of cost or market value. The term 'market value' usually means the current replacement cost, but market value cannot exceed net realisable value nor be less than net realisable value less normal profit margin.

LIFO, average cost or FIFO can be used to calculate the cost of inventory.

B. 'Cost-plus' contracts

ARB 43 (I 78)

Income from cost-plus-fixed-fee contracts should be recognised as income on the basis of such measurements of partial performance as will reflect reasonably assured realisation. Depending upon the circumstances, this may be on the basis of percentage of completion, partial deliveries, billings or some other measure.

C. Other long-term contracts

ARB 45 (Co 4)

When the estimates of the costs to complete a contract and the evaluation of the extent of the progress made towards completing a long-term contract are both reasonably dependable, the percentage-of-completion method is generally preferable to the completed-contract method. Usually all stages of a contract are considered to

UNITED KINGDOM

5.3 STOCKS ('INVENTORY' IN THE US)

A. Cost methods

SSAP 9 (Revised)

Stocks are stated at the lower of cost and net realisable value. Net realisable value is the actual or estimated selling price less any costs to be incurred prior to completion and costs to be incurred in marketing, selling and distributing. The Companies Act 1985 requires the disclosure of significant differences between the valuation and the replacement cost of stock.

FIFO and average cost are methods commonly used to calculate the cost of stocks. Although the Companies Act notes LIFO as a possible valuation method, SSAP 9 (Revised) questions whether this method can give a true and fair view, because it may result in a valuation that bears little relationship to actual cost.

B. Cost-plus contracts

A percentage of completion basis is normally required for all long-term contracts, and any shorter term contracts where profit recognition is essential to the true and fair view. However, other short-term contracts would be dealt with on a completed contracts basis.

C. Other long-term contracts

SSAP 9 (Revised)

Unless there are too many uncertainties in calculating the amount of attributable profit, a percentage-of-completion method should be used for long-term contracts. This would recognise any known inequalities in profitability in various stages of the contract.

The method used in calculating turnover, and hence attributable profit, should be appropriate to the stage of completion of the

UNITED STATES

contribute a uniform profit percentage, and profit is recognised accordingly.

When either a lack of dependable estimates or inherent hazards cause forecasts to be doubtful, the completed-contract method is preferable. The two methods are not considered acceptable alternatives; the circumstances of each contract should dictate the method used.

D. Special valuations

ARB 43 (I 78)

In certain relatively rare and special situations, inventories may be stated at net selling prices, and these may exceed cost. One example is a precious metal that may have a readily determinable market value and no substantial marketing costs. Other examples include industries where the inventory is a fungible (that is, interchangeable) commodity with immediate marketability at widely quoted prices and it is impossible to determine costs, or it is trade custom for inventories to be stated at net selling prices (such as in grain trading companies).

E. Purchase commitments

Provision should be made for net losses on firm purchase commitments of inventory.

UNITED KINGDOM

contract, the business and the industry in which it operates. SSAP 9 (Revised) requires turnover to be recognised on long-term contracts even when no profit is recognised. Income (UK turnover) would not be recognised in the US unless profit or loss was to be recognised as well.

Where the exclusion of profit from the valuation of certain short-term contracts would materially distort the result of successive accounting periods, they should be accounted for as long-term contracts and profit should be recognised. No such recognition is allowed in the US.

D. Special valuations

SSAP 9 (Revised)

The UK standard does not allow stocks to be valued in excess of cost. The use of selling price less an estimated profit margin is acceptable only if it gives a reasonable approximation to actual cost. Certain plantation companies, however, have followed the practice of valuing stocks at net selling prices, and their auditors usually concur. Also, the Companies Act 1985 specifically allows stocks to be shown on the basis of current cost.

E. Purchase commitments

There is no formal requirement regarding purchase commitments, and practice may vary. However, SSAP 18's general requirement for accruing material contingent losses that are likely to occur would normally mean provision should be made.

UNITED STATES

5.4 INVESTMENTS IN ASSOCIATED COMPANIES

APBO 18 (I 82)

Investments in associated companies (normally those where between 20 and 50% voting control is held) should be accounted for by the investor on the equity method of accounting.

If necessary, the financial statements of the associated company should first be adjusted to comply with US GAAP. However, the adjusted accounting policies of that company need not be identical to those of the investor.

The investor's share of the results of the associated company is reported in the income statement net of the associated company's provision for income taxes (that is, taxation). However, it is generally placed in the investor's income statement before the investor's provision for income taxes.

Any goodwill (calculated after considering the fair values of the associated company's net assets) is treated in a similar way to goodwill arising in respect of acquired subsidiaries (see page 22).

UNITED KINGDOM

5.4 INVESTMENTS IN ASSOCIATED COMPANIES

SSAP 1

Investments in associated companies are accounted for in the consolidated financial statements of the investor by the equity method. However, they are normally accounted for in the financial statements of the parent company at cost. In certain cases, investments in associated companies are shown in the parent company's financial statements at a valuation which reflects the parent company's share of the associated company's net assets.

In a similar way to the requirement for subsidiaries, the financial statements of the associated company should be adjusted to achieve reasonable consistency with the accounting practices adopted by the investor's group.

Income from associated companies is recognised in the parent company's financial statements only when received (or receivable) as dividends. In consolidated financial statements, the share of the pre-tax results of an associated company is reported in the consolidated profit before taxation, and the share of the taxation charge is included in the consolidated taxation charge.

Goodwill arising in respect of associated companies is treated similarly to that in respect of subsidiaries. Any goodwill attributable to associated companies that has not been written off or amortised should be disclosed separately in the consolidated financial statements.

UNITED STATES

5.5 MARKETABLE EQUITY SECURITIES

FAS 12 (I 89)

The carrying amount of each portfolio of marketable equity securities shall be the lower of its aggregate cost or market value. However, unrealised losses are accounted for differently, depending upon the portfolio, as explained below.

Current portfolio

Gains and losses realised on the sale of marketable equity securities and the excess of the cost of the portfolio of current marketable equity securities over the market value of that portfolio should be included in the income for the period.

Non-current portfolio

The excess of the cost of the portfolio of non-current marketable equity securities over the market value of that portfolio should be shown separately as a component of shareholders' equity. However, when the decline in the market value of an investment that is included in the non-current portfolio is other than temporary, the necessary write-down shall be accounted for as a realised loss (that is, through the income statement).

UNITED KINGDOM

5.5 MARKETABLE EQUITY SECURITIES

There is no accounting standard in the UK on investments. Under the 'separate valuation' concept in the Companies Act 1985, investments should be valued individually rather than in aggregate.

Current asset investments

There are two acceptable methods of valuation. These are:

- Lower of cost and net realisable value. Losses should be included in income for the period.
- Marking to market. This is a policy where investments held for dealing purposes (which are not limited to marketable equity securities) are included in the accounts at market value. Gains and losses, both realised on sale and unrealised, are included in income for the period.

Non-current investments

Non-current investments may be accounted for at cost or at a valuation. Where valuation exceeds cost, the surplus should be taken to a revaluation reserve (a separate component of shareholders' equity). Where there is a permanent decline in the market value of an investment below cost, then provision should be made in the profit and loss account for the period. Where investments are accounted for at cost, provision is not required where diminutions in value are considered temporary.

UNITED STATES

5.6 CAPITALISATION OF INTEREST COST

FAS 34,58, 62 (I 67)

Interest cost relating to certain types of assets during their acquisition (construction) period must be capitalised.

Assets for which interest capitalisation is required include investments (equity, loans and advances) accounted for by the equity method while the investee has activities in progress necessary to commence its planned principal operations provided that such activities include the use of funds to acquire qualifying assets for its operations.

Specific rules apply as to the determination of amount and period of interest capitalisation.

5.7 INVESTMENT PROPERTIES

Investment properties, like properties held for a company's own use, should be carried at historical cost, and depreciation should be provided on all depreciable assets.

UNITED KINGDOM

5.6 CAPITALISATION OF INTEREST COST

The Companies Act 1985 allows, but does not require, capitalisation of interest on funds borrowed to finance the production of an asset to the extent that it relates to the period of production. The fact that interest has been capitalised and the related amounts should be disclosed. There is no accounting standard and hence there are no specific rules as to how interest capitalisation should be applied.

5.7 INVESTMENT PROPERTIES

SSAP 19

Investment properties should be carried on the balance sheet at open-market value. Any changes in such value should be shown as a movement on an investment revaluation reserve and should not be taken to profit. However, if the reserve moves into deficit, then the deficit should be charged in the profit and loss account. Depreciation should not be provided on investment properties, except for properties held on lease, where amortisation should be provided where the unexpired lease period is 20 years or less, and may be provided where such period is greater than 20 years.

UNITED STATES

5.8 CAPITALISATION OF CERTAIN COMPUTER SOFTWARE COSTS

FAS 86 (R50)

Costs incurred internally in creating a computer software product, which is to be sold, leased or otherwise marketed, must be charged to expense as research and development when incurred until technological feasibility (as defined) has been established. Thereafter, all software production costs must be capitalised and stated at the lower of unamortised cost or net realisable value. Capitalised costs are amortised based on current and estimated future revenue for each product with an annual minimum equal to straight-line amortisation over the remaining estimated economic life of the product.

5.9 INTANGIBLE ASSETS

APBO 17 (I 60)

The cost of intangible assets acquired from other entities should be recorded as an asset. The cost of each type of intangible asset should be amortised over the period that is expected to benefit from that asset. However, the period should not in any case exceed 40 years. Amortisation of intangible assets (including goodwill — see page 22) acquired before 1 November 1970 is not required, except where its value is permanently impaired.

The straight line method of amortisation should be applied unless it can be demonstrated that some other systematic method is more appropriate.

UNITED KINGDOM

5.8 CAPITALISATION OF CERTAIN COMPUTER SOFTWARE COSTS

The UK standard on accounting for research and development does not specifically mention computer software costs. But such costs may be capitalised if they fulfil the criteria for carry-forward (see item 4.11 on page 69).

5.9 INTANGIBLE ASSETS

The Companies Act 1985 specifically requires amortisation of all those intangible assets that have a limited useful economic life (including goodwill — see page 23) and write-down of such assets with permanent decline in value.

The method of amortisation is not specified, and in respect of certain assets such as brands acquired some companies do not amortise the assets, other than where there is a permanent diminution in value, on the grounds that their value does not diminish.

UNITED STATES

5.10 CLASSIFICATION OF LIABILITIES

A. Short term obligations

FAS 6 (B 05)

Short-term obligations are normally included in current liabilities. However, a short-term obligation should be excluded from current liabilities if:

- The company intends to re-finance the obligation on a long-term basis, and
- Long-term financing has been either obtained or arranged before the balance sheet is issued.

B. Long-term obligations that are callable

FAS 78 (B 05)

Long-term obligations that are or will be callable by the creditor either because the debtor's violation of a provision of the debt agreement at the balance sheet date makes the obligation callable or because the violation, if not cured within a specified grace period, will make the obligation callable, are to be classified as current liabilities unless one of the following conditions is met:

- The creditor has waived or subsequently lost the right to demand repayment for more than one year (or operating cycle, if longer) from the balance sheet date.
- For long-term obligations containing a grace period within which the debtor may cure the violation, it is probable that the violation will be cured within that period, thus preventing the obligation from becoming callable.

C. Accruals for loss contingencies ('provisions' in the UK)

ARB 43 (B 05)

Accruals for loss contingencies, (for example, estimated obligations related to product warranties, pending litigation, debt

UNITED KINGDOM

5.10 CLASSIFICATION OF LIABILITIES

A. Short-term obligations

Short-term debt should normally be classified as a current liability, regardless of expected re-financing. However, in practice there are some cases where debt has been re-classified as long-term in circumstances similar to the US criteria.

B. Long-term obligations that are callable

This is not covered by any accounting pronouncement in the UK. However, the Companies Act 1985 states that a loan should be treated as falling due for payment on the earliest date on which the lender could require repayment, if he exercised all options and rights available to him. UK practice would normally require the disclosure of the treatment by way of a note to the financial statements.

C. Provisions ('Accruals for loss contingencies' in the US)

All provisions are classified as non-current. The Companies Act

UNITED STATES

guarantees, etc) are classified as current or long-term based upon the same criteria as all other obligations of the enterprise. That is, all obligations whose liquidation is reasonably expected to require the use of current assets or the creation of other current liabilities are classified as current liabilities.

See page 76 for the classification requirements pertaining to deferred taxes.

UNITED KINGDOM

1985 defines provisions as amounts provided for any liability or loss which is likely to be incurred but uncertain as to amount or as to timing of payment. Movements on provisions must be disclosed.

In practice, exceptions are sometimes made for material provisions expected to be payable currently which may require separate current classification in order to present a 'true and fair view'.

Deferred taxation is considered a provision for UK purposes.

UNITED STATES

5.11   RESTRUCTURING OF DEBT

FAS 15 (D 22)

The following accounting treatment is required by debtors and by creditors for transactions relating to the restructuring of debt when the debtor has difficulties in fulfilling its obligations:

- *Transfers of assets or equity in full settlement of obligation.* Debtors should recognise the difference between the fair value and the carrying amount of any asset transferred as a gain or loss on the disposition of assets. Debtors also should recognise as a gain any excess of the carrying amount of the obligation settled over the fair value of the asset transferred, or the fair value of the equity interest granted, in settlement of the obligation. Likewise, creditors should recognise as a loss the excess of the carrying amount of the obligation settled over the fair value of the assets or equity interest received.

- *Modification of terms.* Debtors and creditors should account for such modifications prospectively by reducing the effective rate of interest generated under the new payment terms. Gains and losses should be recognised only if the total revised payments are less than the balance of the debt.

Disclosures are required by debtors and creditors in these situations, including the nature and the terms of the restructuring, gains and losses recognised, etc.

UNITED KINGDOM

5.11 RESTRUCTURING OF DEBT

There are no accounting requirements for the restructuring of debt.
Practice varies.

UNITED STATES

5.12 PREMIUM AND DISCOUNT ON LIABILITIES

APBO 12 (I 69)

The 'interest method' of amortisation is regarded as an appropriate method of accounting for both the premium or discount on the debt and the expenses incurred in raising that debt. Under this method, the difference between the net proceeds from the issue of debt and the amount repayable on redemption should be amortised over the period during which the debt is outstanding so as to result in a constant effective rate of amortisation based on the aggregate remaining balance of debt and unamortised premium or discount and expenses at the beginning of each period.

5.13 LIABILITIES WITH EQUITY OR CONVERSION FEATURES

APBO 14 (C 08, D 10)

When debt securities are issued with detachable stock purchase warrants, the amount of the proceeds that relates to those warrants should be accounted for as if they were paid-in capital. The opinion specifies the manner in which the proceeds should be allocated between the debt element and the warrants. Proceeds from the issuing of convertible debt, however, should be accounted for entirely as liabilities. No portion of those proceeds should be attributed to the conversion feature.

UNITED KINGDOM

5.12   PREMIUM AND DISCOUNT ON LIABILITIES

Although there is no mandatory accounting treatment, a Technical Release issued by the ICAEW in 1987 (TR 677) recommends that where the cost of repaying loan capital is greater than the proceeds of the issue, the difference should be charged to the profit and loss account in a manner equivalent to the US. This is now considered best accounting practice for deep discount bonds.

Debt issue expense is normally written off immediately, either to share premium account if permissible or to profit and loss account.

5.13   LIABILITIES WITH EQUITY OR CONVERSION FEATURES

The above mentioned TR 677 recommends that proceeds from the issue of bonds with detachable warrants should be split, and the latter treated as capital. However, actual practice varies and all proceeds relating to borrowings may be accounted for as liabilities, the effect of any stock warrants being disclosed in a note.

UNITED STATES

5.14 TREASURY STOCK

ARB 43 (C 23)

A corporation that acquires its own capital shares generally should not account for such shares as assets but as adjustments to shareholders' equity, as follows:

- If the shares were acquired for retirement, any excess of the purchase price over the par value should be either charged against retained earnings or allocated between capital surplus and retained earnings. Any excess of the par value over the purchase price should be credited to capital surplus.
- If the shares were acquired for other purposes, either the above accounting treatment may be applied or the cost of such acquired shares (referred to as 'treasury shares', or 'treasury stock') may be shown as a separate deduction from shareholders' equity.

  Any gains on resale of treasury shares should be credited to capital surplus. Losses may be charged to capital surplus to the extent of previous gains. Otherwise, they should be charged to retained earnings.

5.15 DIVIDENDS

Dividends declared are shown as a liability and as a deduction from retained earnings. They are not so shown, however, until they have been formally declared, because dividends are not attributable to any particular period's earnings in the US.

UNITED KINGDOM

5.14 OWN SHARES

Accounting for the purchase by a company of its own shares is not presently covered by any UK accounting pronouncements. However, the accounting treatment follows the law. Companies that acquire their own capital shares are generally required formally to cancel such shares. This reduces issued capital, but not authorised capital. Generally, the purchase must be made out of distributable profits and a statutory capital redemption reserve must be established to maintain capital equivalent to the nominal value of shares purchased or redeemed.

In the relatively rare cases where the holding of such shares for a short period is permitted (for example, through gifts or forfeitures) they may, under the Companies Act 1985, be accounted for as investments.

The term 'treasury stock' is not widely used in the UK, 'own shares' being the UK term.

5.15 DIVIDENDS

Dividends paid and proposed are usually shown on the face of the profit and loss account as an appropriation of the current year's earnings. Proposed dividends are provided on the basis of recommendation by the directors and may include dividends that are subject to subsequent approval by shareholders before they are declared. Proposed dividends are shown as a current liability and must be separately disclosed either on the face of the balance sheet or in the notes to the financial statements.

UNITED STATES

5.16   STOCK DIVIDENDS ('SCRIP DIVIDENDS' IN THE UK)

ARB 43 (C 20)

A company's distribution of its own capital shares to its shareholders without receiving consideration in return may be either a 'stock dividend' or a 'stock split-up', depending on the circumstances.

A stock dividend is a distribution that is prompted mainly by a desire to give the shareholders a part of the company's earnings without giving up assets needed in the business. In these cases, retained earnings equal to the fair value of the shares distributed should be 'capitalised' (that is, transferred to share capital and share premium accounts).

A stock split-up, or stock split, is a distribution prompted mainly by a desire to increase the number of outstanding shares and reduce the market price, and so improve the marketability of the shares, etc. In these cases, retained earnings need not be capitalised other than to the extent necessary to meet legal requirements.

Although no single percentage is used as a standard for determining whether a distribution is a stock dividend or a stock split, generally a distribution of less than 20-25% would be presumed to be a stock dividend. Distributions of more than 20-25% are presumed to be stock split-ups, unless this presumption is destroyed by frequent distributions.

UNITED KINGDOM

5.16 SCRIP DIVIDENDS ('STOCK DIVIDENDS' IN THE US)

Scrip dividends are a recent innovation in the UK, where some companies give shareholders the alternative of electing to receive new shares instead of the usual cash dividends. There is no accounting pronouncement on the subject and there are two methods of dealing with it. Proposed dividends are initially provided on the basis of the cash option. One method is to credit share capital and share premium with the value of the cash dividend option in respect of shares issued in lieu of cash. The other method is to credit revenue reserves with the cash equivalent of the shares issued, and to treat the shares issued as a bonus issue. That is, only the nominal value of the shares issued is recognised, which is treated as a capitalisation of share premium account or other reserves.

The UK counterpart to a stock split-up is a bonus or scrip issue of shares. This is dealt with by a capitalisation of reserves (share premium, revaluation reserve or any other available reserves) to the extent of the nominal value of new shares issued.

COMMON ABBREVIATIONS

AICPA American Institute of Certified Public Accountants, the US national body to which practising and some non-practising certified public accountants belong.

APC Auditing Practices Committee, which develops UK auditing standards and guidelines, which are initially published as exposure drafts. The final standards and guidelines are approved and subsequently published by the three Institutes of Chartered Accountants, the Chartered Association of Certified Accountants and CIPFA.

APB, APBO Accounting Principles Board, the professional body established within the AICPA during 1959 to 1973 to issue authoritative accounting pronouncements. These pronouncements are referred to as APB Opinions or APBOs.

ARB Accounting Research Bulletin, the US accounting pronouncements issued by the AICPA prior to the tenure of the APB.

ASC Accounting Standards Committee, the UK/Irish body established to develop accounting pronouncements in the UK and Ireland.

CACA Chartered Association of Certified Accountants, one of the six UK and Irish accountancy bodies.

CCA Current Cost Accounting, a concept recognised in the UK and set out in the ASC's SSAP No. 16 (now withdrawn). It departs from the historical cost concept to a concept of accounting for specific price changes in a business.

CCAB Consultative Committee of Accountancy Bodies, a committee formed by the six UK and Irish accountancy bodies.

CIMA Chartered Institute of Management Accountants, a national body of UK and Irish accountants primarily engaged in commerce and industry. They are roughly equivalent to the NAA in the US.

CIPFA Chartered Institute of Public Finance and Accountancy whose members generally work in the public sector in the UK.

CPA Certified Public Accountant, the recognised professional qualification of an accountant in the US. A CPA is the US equivalent of a UK or an Irish chartered accountant. Each state has its own body of CPAs and sets its own licensing requirements. The CPA examination, however, is a uniform examination developed and administered by the AICPA simultaneously throughout the US.

CA, ACA, FCA Chartered Accountant, the main recognised professional qualification of an accountant in the UK and Ireland. A chartered accountant is the UK equivalent of a US CPA. The 'CA' designation is used by Scottish chartered accountants. Chartered accountants in England and Wales use the designations 'ACA' (which means Associate of the Institute of Chartered Accountants in England and Wales) and, generally after five years' membership, 'FCA' (which means Fellow of the Institute of Chartered Accountants in England and Wales). Chartered accountants in Ireland use similar designations. Members of the relevant Institutes are, along with members of ACCA, qualified to act as auditors under the Companies Act 1985.

ED Exposure Draft of a proposed Statement of Standard Accounting Practice (SSAP — see below). This abbreviation is generally used in the UK but not in the US. The EDs are numbered according to the sequence in which they are issued, and they are issued for discussion and consideration for a period.

EITF Emerging Issues Task Force, established in 1984 by the FASB to aid in identifying emerging issues that may ultimately require action by the FASB. Although the findings of the EITF are not strictly US GAAP, when a consensus is reached on an issue it is followed by most US companies.

FASB Financial Accounting Standards Board, the US accounting body authorised since 1973 to issue authoritative accounting pronouncements. These pronouncements include Statements on Financial Accounting Standards (FAS) and Accounting Interpretations. FASB Technical Bulletins are issued by the staff of the FASB.

FORM 10-K An annual reporting form (containing audited financial statements and other financial information) required to be filed by US companies reporting to the Securities and Exchange Commission in the United States. The Form 10-Q is the quarterly report form. Foreign companies with such reporting requirements are required to file Form 20-F annually.

GAAP Generally Accepted Accounting Principles, which encompass those accounting principles and practices that are generally regarded as acceptable in practice in the US. GAAP include the accounting statements and the interpretations of the FASB, the opinions of the APB, and ARBs, as well as practices that have obtained acceptance through general usage.

GAAS Generally Accepted Auditing Standards, which comprise the basic standards and the underlying objectives and procedures (set out in Statements on Auditing Standards) that must be followed by US auditors in the US (and any other auditors reporting on the basis of US GAAS).

ICA   Institute of Chartered Accountants (see CA).

NAA   National Association of Accountants, a national
             accounting organisation in the US, primarily for
             accountants engaged in industry or government, but its
             members also include many practising CPAs and
             academicians.

PLC   Public Limited Company, a UK company limited by
             shares which is registered as a public company.
             However, a PLC need not be a quoted company.

REGULA-   Identifies the information required to be disclosed in
TION S-X   financial statements that are filed with the SEC (see
             below). Regulation S-X was first published by the SEC
             in 1940, but it is continually updated.

SEC   Securities and Exchange Commission, a US
             government regulatory agency set up by the Securities
             Exchange Act of 1934 to administer the Securities Acts
             of 1933 and 1934.

SOP   Statements of Position issued by the AICPA as guidance
             on particular accounting issues. Although the AICPA's
             views are not enforceable they are generally followed
             by the accountancy profession. SOPs have been
             generally endorsed by FASB for purposes of justifying
             an accounting change.

SORP   Statement of Recommended Practice, developed in the
             public interest to set out current best accounting practice
             on subjects that have a limited scope. The ASC develops
             and issues SORPs, or they may be developed by
             specialised industry groups.

SSAP   Statement of Standard Accounting Practice, the
             authoritative accounting pronouncements issued in the
             UK by the ASC (see above), after approval by the six
             member bodies of CCAB, and required to be followed
             by all companies (except as designated) whose financial
             statements are supposed to give a true and fair view.

COOPERS & LYBRAND DELOITTE UK OFFICES

London — City
Plumtree Court
London EC4A 4HT
Tel: (071) 583 5000
Fax: (071) 822 4652

P.O. Box 207
128 Queen Victoria Street
London EC4P 4JX
Tel: (071) 583 5000
Fax: (071) 248 3623

P.O. Box 198
Hillgate House
26 Old Bailey
London EC4M 7PL
Tel: (071) 583 5000
Fax: (071) 236 2367

London — West
Harman House
1 George Street
Uxbridge UB8 1QQ
Tel: (0895) 73333
Fax: (0895) 56413

Aberdeen
32 Albyn Place
Aberdeen AB1 1YL
Tel: (0224) 592373
Fax: (0224) 576183

Armagh
3-5 Market Street
Armagh BT61 7BW
Tel: (0861) 522695
Fax: (0861) 526820

Bangor
20 Hamilton Road
Bangor BT20 4LE
Tel: (0247) 466516
Fax: (0247) 270603

Belfast
Northern Bank House
10 High Street
Belfast BT1 2BL
Tel: (0232) 246969
Fax: (0232) 232900

Fanum House
108 Great Victoria Street
Belfast BT2 7AX
Tel: (0232) 245454
Fax: (0232) 242416

18 Orby Link
Castlereagh
Belfast BT 5HW
Tel: (0232) 799096
Fax: (0232) 799110

Yorkshire House
10 Donegal Sq. South,
Donegal
Belfast BT1 5JD
Tel: (0232) 233519

Birmingham
43 Temple Row
Birmingham B2 5JT
Tel: (021) 233 1100
Fax: (021) 200 4040

35 Newhall Street
Birmingham B3 3DX
Tel: (021) 200 2828
Fax: (021) 200 2829

Blackburn
Parkgates
52A Preston New Road
Blackburn BB2 6AH
Tel: (0254) 675327
Fax: (0254) 680827

Bournemouth
Hill House
Richmond Hill
Bournemouth BH2 6HS
Tel: (0202) 294621
Fax: (0202) 26978

Bristol
66 Queen Square
Bristol BS1 4JP
Tel: (0272) 292791
    (0272) 260514
Fax: (0272) 307008
    (0272) 290810

Cambridge
Abacus House
Castle Park
Gloucester Street
Cambridge CB3 0AN
Tel: (0223) 323881
Fax: (0223) 64036

Mount Pleasant House
Huntingdon Road
Cambridge CB3 0BL
Tel: (0223) 314992
Fax: (0223) 61156

Cardiff
Tudor House
16 Cathedral Road
Cardiff CF1 6PN
Tel: (0222) 239944
Fax: (0222) 238838

Churchill House
Churchill Way
Cardiff CF1 4XQ
Tel: (0222) 237000
Fax: (0222) 223361

Croydon
Melrose House
42 Dingwall Road
Croydon CR0 2NE
Tel: (081) 681 5252
Fax: (081) 760 0897

Dungannon
16 Northland Road
Dungannon BT71 6AP
Tel: (08637) 22726
Fax: (08637) 27324

Edinburgh
George House
126 George Street
Edinburgh EH2 4JZ
Tel: (031) 226 2595
Fax: (031) 226 2692

P.O. Box 90
25 Abercromby Place
Edinburgh EH3 6QS
Tel: (031) 557 3333
Fax: (031) 556 2751

Enniskillen
9 Townhall Street
Enniskillen BT74 7BA
Tel: (0365) 322617
Fax: (0365) 322649

Glasgow
Kintyre House
209 West George Street
Glasgow G2 2LW
Tel: (041) 248 2644
Tel: Cork Gully:
    (041) 226 4894
Fax: (041) 221 8256

Gloucester
Lennox House
Beaufort Buildings
Spa Road
Gloucester GL1 1XD
Tel: (0452) 423031
Fax: (0452) 300699

Irvine
Galt House
31 Bank Street
Irvine KA12 0AJ
Tel: (0294) 78046
Fax: (0294) 75692

King's Lynn
11 King Street
King's Lynn PE30 1ET
Tel: (0553) 761316
Fax: (0553) 766454

Larne
20 Upper Main Street
Larne BT40 1SX
Tel: (0574) 75733
Fax: (0574) 60038

Leeds
Albion Court
5 Albion Place
Leeds LS1 6JP
Tel: (0532) 431343
Fax: (0532) 424009

Cloth Hall Court
Infirmary Street
Leeds LS1 2HT
Tel: (0532) 455166
Fax: (0532) 434567

Leicester
Abacus House
32 Friar Lane
Leicester LE1 5RA
Tel: (0533) 518164
Fax: (0533) 536929

Liverpool
State House
22 Dale Street
Liverpool L2 4UH

Richmond House
1 Rumford Place
Liverpool L3 9QS
Tel: (051) 227 4242
Fax: (051) 227 4575

Maidstone
Orchard House
10 Albion Place
Maidstone ME14 5DZ
Tel: (0622) 672961
Fax: (0622) 58071

Manchester
Abacus Court
6 Minshull Street
Manchester M1 3ED
Tel: (061) 236 9191
Fax: (061) 247 4000

Bank House
Charlotte Street
Manchester M14BX
Tel: (061) 236 9565
Fax: (061) 228 3920

Middlesbrough
Church House
Grange Road
Middlesbrough TS1 2LR
Tel: (0642) 241001
Fax: (0642) 222330

Milton Keynes
Central Business Exchange
Midsummer Boulevard
Central Milton Keynes
MK9 2DF
Tel: (0908) 690064
Fax: (0908) 690065

Newcastle upon Tyne
Archbold House
Archbold Terrace
Newcastle upon Tyne
NE2 1DQ
Tel: (091) 281 4911
Fax: (091) 281 7492

Hadrian House
Higham Place
Newcastle upon Tyne
NE1 8BP
Tel: (091) 261 2121
Fax: (091) 232 6534

Northampton
Oriel House
55 Sheep Street
Northampton NN1 2NF
Tel: (0604) 230770
Fax: (0604) 238001

Norwich
The Atrium
St. George's Street
Norwich NR3 1AG
Tel: (0603) 615244
Fax: (0603) 631060

Nottingham
Cumberland House
35 Park Row
Nottingham NG1 6FY
Tel: (0602) 419066
Tel: Cork Gully:
     (0602) 410192
Fax: (0602) 470862

Omagh
43 Market Street
Omagh BT78 1EE
Tel: (0662) 246100
Tax: (0662) 246283

Plymouth
Mutley House
23 Princess Street
Plymouth PL1 2HE
Tel: (0752) 267441
Fax: (0752) 673514

Portadown
43 High Street
Portadown BT62 1HY
Tel: (0762) 333718
Fax: (0762) 350201

Reading
9 Greyfriars Road
Reading RG1 1JG
Tel: (0734) 597111
Fax: (0734) 607700

Sheffield
1 East Parade
Sheffield S1 2ET
Tel: (0742) 729141
Fax: (0742) 752573

Southampton
5 Town Quay
Southampton SO9 1ZG
Tel: (0703) 632772
Fax: (0703) 330493

Wheatsheaf House
24 Bernard Street
Southampton SO9 1QL
Tel: (0703) 634521
Fax: (0703) 226657

Swansea
Princess House
Princess Way
Swansea SA1 5LH
Tel: (0792) 473691
Fax: (0792) 476857

P.O. Box 60
Midland Bank
   Chambers
Castle Square
Swansea SA1 1DU
Tel: (0792) 475777
Fax: (0792) 474428

Warwick
Vanguard Centre
University of Warwick
   Science Park
Sir William Lyons Road
Coventry CV4 7EZ
Tel: (0203) 417585
Fax: (0203) 411151

COOPERS & LYBRAND US OFFICES

National
1251 Avenue of the
  Americas
New York
New York 10020
Tel: 212 536 2000
Fax: 212 536 3500

Akron Ohio
800 Akron Center Plaza
PO Box 80538
Akron
Ohio 44308
Tel: 216 253 7100
Fax: 216 434 5505

Albany New York
State Street Center
80 State Street
Albany
New York 12207
Tel: 518 462 2030
Fax: 518 462 2045

Anchorage Alaska
550 West Seventh Avenue
Suite 600
Anchorage
Alaska 99501-3558
Tel: 907 274 3602
Fax: 907 272 6614

Atlanta Georgia
1100 Campanile Bulding
1155 Peachtree Street
Atlanta
Georgia 30309
Tel: 404 870 1100
Fax: 404 870 1239

Aurora Illinois
PO Box 910
Aurora
Illinois 60507
Tel: 708 859 3530
Fax: 708 859 2970

Austin Texas
600 Congress Avenue
1800 One American Center
Austin
Texas 78701
Tel: 512 477 1300
Fax: 512 477 8681

Baltimore Maryland
Redwood Tower
217 E. Redwood Street
Baltimore
Maryland 21202
Tel: 301 783 7600
Fax: 301 783 7680

Birmingham Alabama
1901 6th Avenue North
Suite 1600
Birmingham
Alabama 35203
Tel: 205 252 8400
Fax: 205 252 7776

Boise Idaho
1200 Idaho First Plaza
Boise
Idaho 83702
Tel: 208 343 4801
Fax: 208 343 6787

Boston Massachusetts
One Post Office Square
Boston
Massachusetts 02109
Tel: 617 574 5000
Fax: 617 542 1297

Burlington Massachusetts
Center for Manufacturing
  Technology
144 Middlesex Turnpike
Burlington
Massachusetts 01803
Tel: 617 229 1000
Fax: 617 229 1016

Charlotte North Carolina
1850 Charlotte Plaza
Charlotte
North Carolina 28244
Tel: 704 375 8414
Fax: 704 347 1601

Chicago Illinois
203 North La Salle Street
Chicago
Illinois 60601
Tel: 312 701 5500
Fax: 312 701 6533/6534

**Chicago Board of Trade
  Illinois**
141 West Jackson Boulevard
Suite 1520-A
Chicago
Illinois 60604
Tel: 312 408 4100
Fax: 312 408 4141

Cincinnati Ohio
1500 Atrium One
201 East Fourth Street
Cincinnati
Ohio 45202
Tel: 513 651 4000
Fax: 513 768 4599

Cleveland Ohio
1500 One Cleveland Center
1375 East Ninth Street
Cleveland
Ohio 44114-1700
Tel: 216 241 4380
Fax: 216 575 0170

Columbia South Carolina
Suite 1100
1901 Main Street
Mail Code 102
Columbia
South Carolina 29201-2435
Tel: 803 765 2112
Fax: 803 765 1972

Columbus Ohio
100 East Broad Street
Columbus
Ohio 43215
Tel: 614 225 8700
Fax: 614 224 1044

Dallas Texas
1999 Bryan Street
Suite 3000
Dallas
Texas 75201
Tel: 214 754 5000
Fax: 214 953 0669

Dayton Ohio
2080 Kettering Tower
Dayton
Ohio 45423
Tel: 513 223 5185
Fax: 513 222 9227

Denver Colorado
370 Seventeenth Street
Suite 3300
Denver
Colorado 80202-5633
Tel: 303 573 2800
Fax: 303 623 2408

Des Moines Iowa
Suite 2800
801 Grand
Des Moines
Iowa 50309
Tel: 515 282 9141
Fax: 515 282 0155

Detroit Michigan
400 Renaissance Center
Detroit
Michigan 48243
Tel: 313 446 7100
Fax: 313 446 7117

Elkhart Indiana
Suite 407
121 West Franklin Street
Elkhart
Indiana 46516
Tel: 219 294 7441
Fax: 219 293 8923

El Paso Texas
MBank Plaza
Suite 1600
El Paso
Texas 79901
Tel: 915 545 5800
Fax: 915 545 5888

Eugene Oregon
PO Box 1600
Eugene
Oregon 97440-1600
Tel: 503 485 1600
Fax: 503 485 5044

Fort Lauderdale Forida
One Financial Plaza
Suite 1900
Fort Lauderdale
Florida 33394
Tel: 305 764 7111
Fax: 305 525 4453

Fort Myers Florida
PO Box A
Fort Myers
Florida 33902
Tel: 813 433 0888
Fax: 813 433 8762

Fort Wayne Indiana
490 Lincoln Bank Tower
Fort Wayne
Indiana 46802
Tel: 219 423 1531
Fax: 219 426 7870

Fort Worth Texas
301 Commerce Street
City Center II
Suite 1900
Forth Worth
Texas 76102-4119
Tel: 817 332 2243
Fax: 817 332 2710

Grand Rapids Michigan
509 Waters Building
Grand Rapids
Michigan 49503
Tel: 616 458 7700
Fax: 616 454 6375

Harrisburg Pennsylvania
5 North Fifth Street
Suite 500
Harrisburg
Pennsylvania 17101
Tel: 717 231 5900
Fax: 717 232 5672

Hartford Connecticut
280 Trumbull Street
Hartford
Connecticut 06103-3598
Tel: 203 722 1900
Fax: 203 722 1991

Honolulu Hawaii
Suite 2500
Pacific Tower
Bishop Square
1001 Bishop Street
Honolulu
Hawaii 96813-3668
Tel: 808 531 3400
Fax: 808 531 3433

Houston Texas
1100 Louisiana
Suite 4100
Houston
Texas 77002
Tel: 713 757 5200
Fax: 713 757 5249

Indianapolis Indiana
2900 One American Square
Box 82002
Indianapolis
Indiana 46282-0002
Tel: 317 639 4161
Fax: 317 638 5028

Jacksonville Florida
1300 First Union Building
Jacksonville
Florida 32202
Tel: 904 354 0671
Fax: 904 354 3578

Kansas City Missouri
City Center Square
Suite 900
1100 Main
Kansas City
Missouri 64105-2175
Tel: 816 474 6800
Fax: 816 472 1069

Knoxville Tennessee
1600 Plaza Tower
Knoxville
Tennessee 37929
Tel: 615 524 4000
Fax: 615 524 0841

Lexington Kentucky
1400 First Security Plaza
Lexington
Kentucky 40507-1386
Tel: 606 255 3366
Fax: 606 254 2594

Lincoln Nebraska
Cornhusker Square
301 South 13 Suite 700
Lincoln
Nebraska 68508
Tel: 402 475 7633
Fax: 402 475 2093

Long Island New York
225 Broad Hollow Road
Melville
Long Island
New York 11747
Tel: 516 753 2700
Fax: 516 420 9261

Los Angeles California
PO Box 17919
Los Angeles
California 90017-0919
Tel: 213 481 1000
Fax: 213 482 6363

Louisville Kentucky
3500 First National Tower
101 South Fifth Street
Louisville
Kentucky 40202
Tel: 502 589 6100
Fax: 502 589 1253

Lubbock Texas
First National Bank
  Building
1500 Broadway
13th Floor
Lubbock
Texas 79401
Tel: 806 744 3333
Fax: 806 747 2106

Lynchburg Virginia
PO Box 10189
Lynchburg
Virginia 24506
Tel: 804 846 2755
Fax: 804 845 0999

**Manchester
New Hampshire**
PO Box 5080
Manchester
New Hampshire 03108
Tel: 603 669 2200
Fax: 603 624 8351

Maui Hawaii
202 Wailuku Townhouse
  Building
2158 Main Street
Wailuku, Maui
Hawaii 96793
Tel: 808 244 5527
Fax: 808 244 9397

Memphis Tennessee
1000 Morgan-Keegan Tower
Fifty North Front Street
Memphis
Tennessee 38103
Tel: 901 529 1100
Fax: 901 523 2045

Menlo Park California
Suite 150/Building 2
3000 Sand Hill Road
Menlo Park
California 94025
Tel: 408 295 1020
Fax: 415 854 3623

Miami Florida
5959 Blue Lagoon Drive
Miami
Florida 33126
Tel: 305 263 8200
Fax: 305 263 8221

Midland Texas
1900 Wilco Building
415 West Wall Street
Midland
Texas 79701
Tel: 915 687 2000
Fax: 915 683 9126

Milwaukee Wisconsin
The 411 East Wisconsin
  Building
Milwaukee
Wisconsin 53202
Tel: 414 271 3200
Fax: 414 271 7820

**Minneapolis/St Paul
  Minnesota**
1000 TCF Tower
121 South Eighth Street
Minneapolis
Minnesota 55402
Tel: 612 370 9300
Fax: 612 370 9395

New Orleans Louisiana
Suite 2800
One Poydras Plaza
639 Loyola Avenue
New Orleans
Louisiana 70113
Tel: 504 529 2700
Fax: 504 529 1439

New York New York
1251 Avenue of the
  Americas
New York
New York 10020
Tel: 212 536 2000
Fax: 212 536 3500

Newport Beach California
4675 MacArthur Court
Suite 1600
Newport Beach
California 92660
Tel: 714 251 7200
Fax: 714 476 8020

Newport News Virginia
11832 Rock Landing Drive
Newport News
Virginia 23606
Tel: 804 873 0030
Fax: 804 873 3052

Norfolk Virginia
Suite 800
World Trade Center
Norfolk
Virginia 23510
Tel: 804 625 2535
Fax: 804 622 6849

Oakland California
1999 Harrison
Oakland
California 94612
Tel: 415 834 5400
Fax: 415 839 6834

Oklahoma City Oklahoma
100 North Broadway
Suite 3300
Oklahoma City
Oklahoma 73102
Tel: 405 236 5800
Fax: 405 232 5238

Omaha Nebraska
600 Woodmen Tower
Omaha
Nebraska 68102-2087
Tel: 402 344 4545
Fax: 402 345 9521

Orlando Florida
501 North Orange
  Avenue
Orlando
Florida 32801
Tel: 407 843 1190
Fax: 407 423 2949

Parsippany New Jersey
Morris County Financial
  Center
One Sylvan Way
Parsippany
New Jersey 07054
Tel: 201 829 9000
Fax: 201 829 9313

**Philadelphia
  Pennsylvania**
2400 Eleven Penn Center
Philadelphia
Pennsylvania19103
Tel: 215 963 8000
Fax: 215 963 8700

Phoenix Arizona
2901 North Central
  Avenue
Phoenix
Arizona 85012-2755
Tel: 602 280 1800
Fax: 602 280 1999

Pittsburgh Pennsylvania
35th Floor
600 Grant Street
Pittsburgh
Pennsylvania 15219
Tel: 412 355 8000
Fax: 412 355 8089

Portland Maine
130 Middle Street
Portland
Maine 04101
Tel: 207 774 4541
Fax: 207 774 1297

Portland Oregon
2700 First Interstate Bank
  Tower
1300 SW Fifth Avenue
Portland
Oregon 97201-5687
Tel: 503 227 8600
Fax: 503 224 1579

Princeton New Jersey
PO Box 5258
Princeton
New Jersey 08540
Tel: 609 452 0540
Fax: 609 452 0177

Raleigh North Carolina
2626 Glenwood Avenue
Suite 300
Raleigh
North Carolina 27608
Tel: 919 781 8941
Fax: 919 782 8515

Richmond Virginia
1200 Riverfront Plaza
901 East Bynd Street
Richmond
Virginia 23219
Tel: 804 643 0234
Fax: 804 780 1753

Rochester New York
Suite 1000
Two State Street
Rochester
New York 14614
Tel: 716 546 5295
Fax: 716 546 1364

Rockford Illinois
6000 East State Street
Rockford
Illinois 61108
Tel: 815 394 0300
Fax: 815 394 5499

Sacramento California
555 Capitol Mall
Suite 1190
Sacramento
California 95814-4683
Tel: 916 441 4334
Fax: 916 444 8988

St Louis Missouri
One Metropolitan Square
Suite 2200
St Louis
Missouri 63102-2737
Tel: 314 436 3200
Fax: 314 241 3371

Salt Lake City Utah
Suite 1700
Beneficial Life Tower
36 South State Street
Salt Lake City
Utah 84111
Tel: 801 531 9666
Fax: 801 363 7371

San Diego California
Suite 1600
401 West A Street
San Diego
California 92101
Tel: 619 232 8000
Fax: 619 235 0637

San Francisco California
333 Market Street
San Francisco
California 94105
Tel: 415 957 3000
Fax: 415 957 3394

San Jose California
Ten Almaden Boulevard
Suite 1600
San Jose
California 95113
Tel: 408 295 1020
Fax: 408 292 1382

Seattle Washington
Suite 1800
First Interstate Center
999 Third Avenue
Seattle
Washington 98104-4098
Tel: 206 622 8700
Fax: 206 628 8147

**Sherman Oaks
California**
American Savings Plaza
15260 Ventura
Boulevard
Suite 2200
Sherman Oaks
California 91403
Tel: 818 905 0605
Fax: 818 981 3839

South Bend Indiana
PO Box 4157
South Bend
Indiana 46634-4157
Tel: 219 234 4021
Fax: 219 288 0085

Spokane Washington
West 601 Riverside
Avenue
Suite 1600
Spokane
Washington 99201-0640
Tel: 509 455 9300
Fax: 509 838 5459

**Springfield
Massachusetts**
PO Box 59
Springfield
Massachusetts 01101
Tel: 413 781 7200
Fax: 413 733 2195

Stamford Connecticut
PO Box 10108
Stamford
Connecticut 06904-2108
Tel: 203 326 8400
Fax: 203 323 0771

Syracuse New York
One Lincoln Center
Syracuse
New York 13202
Tel: 315 474 8541
Fax: 315 474 0259

Tampa Florida
101 East Kennedy
Boulevard
Suite 1500
Tampa
Florida 33602
Tel: 813 229 0221
Fax: 813 229 3646

Tucson Arizona
33 North Stone Avenue
1900 Security Pacific
Bank
Tucson
Arizona 85701
Tel: 602 792 3660
Fax: 602 791 2154

Tulsa Oklahoma
1400 Mid-Continent
Tower
401 South Boston
Tulsa
Oklahoma 74103
Tel: 918 582 6404
Fax: 918 582 3327

**Valley Forge
Pennsylvania**
600 Lee Road
Suite 200
Wayne
Pennsylvania 19087
Tel: 215 993 3800
Fax: 215 640 3790

**Washington District of
Columbia**
1800 M Street NW
Washington DC 20036
Tel: 202 822 4000
Fax: 202 296 8933

**West Palm Beach
Florida**
1675 Palm Beach
Lakes Boulevard
West Palm Beach
Florida 33401-9986
Tel: 407 686 9300
Fax: 407 683 4716